KENNETH WELLS

WOODEN PUZZLES AND GAMES

Intriguing projects you can make

 Sterling Publishing Co., Inc.   New York

This book is dedicated to the unknown originators of many of the games and puzzles presented in it. Their ingenuity has given fun and frustration to millions.

Published in 1983 by
Sterling Publishing Co., Inc.
Two Park Avenue
New York, N.Y. 10016

Printed in Great Britain

ISBN 0-8069-7736-1 paper
ISBN 0-8069-5490-6 trade

Published by arrangement with David & Charles Ltd.
This edition available in the United States, Canada and the Philippine Islands only.

CONTENTS

INTRODUCTION

Man's fascination with puzzles and games of all kinds is timeless, and seems to be on the increase. The proliferation of puzzle magazines, of video games, and the fantastic success of Professor Erno Rubik's cube, all seem to confirm this fact; a reaction, perhaps, against the passivity of much of today's merely visual entertainment.

This book presents fifteen puzzles and six games, many familiar, some less so, all adapted to appeal to the craftsman of today. It is not necessary to be a skilled cabinet maker to tackle these projects, nor are they so simple that they do not present something of a challenge. Only relatively basic woodworking techniques are required (no complicated joints are incorporated) and, harnessed to careful workmanship, really pleasing results can be achieved. An advantage for today's woodworkers, with so many demands on their time, is that the compact size of many individual puzzles allows them to be completed in one leisurely day's work.

In most cases, the construction of the projects is described and illustrated using hand tools, but it is obvious where power tools can be substituted to speed up the work. Black-and-white photographs accompany each project, and are used not only to show specific procedures or techniques, but also to illustrate the general progress of the project. Most of the drawings are diagrammatic, or isometric, because these give more information, and are more readily understood, than the projection type.

Many of the puzzles and games have been fashioned from beautiful, semi-precious woods. Such woods are rewarding to work with, but are rarely feasible to use for larger projects because of their cost.

Unlike most woodworking books, mainly presenting worthy, practical designs, this one does more; it offers woodworking for pleasure, firstly in creating the puzzles and games themselves, and secondly in solving and playing them.

Measurements

Metric and imperial measurements are given, the latter in brackets, but they are not interchangeable; projects should be made entirely in one or the other. 'Bilingual' craftsmen, those who perhaps use metric small measurements and imperial large ones, will find that this system is not feasible for these projects. Many larger sizes are multiples of smaller ones and although the difference between, say 20mm and ¾in is insignificant in itself, it can become of considerable importance when the product of several such measurements is involved.

4

1 TOOLS

The popularity of machine tools today has altered the composition of the craftsman's hand tool kit. Some items, considered essential only a decade or two ago, are now rarely purchased or have been withdrawn from the tool manufacturer's catalogue. However, many are still with us, and will be as long as enough craftsmen enjoy practising their skills. Most essential tools are included in this list, although it is not comprehensive enough to include *every* tool required to make *every* puzzle and game. Neither does it include those basic tools that are already to be found in most households.

Good tools last at least a lifetime, and it is, therefore, a wise investment to purchase only those manufactured by a familiar name with a reputation to maintain. Other tools, though superficially identical, may be made of inferior materials, and the all-important heat treatment of the blades may also be faulty. Such tools, instead of giving pleasure and good service, offer only frustration until they are discarded. The old adage 'you get what you pay for' is not always true today but, where tools are concerned, it can be unwise to ignore such advice.

Rule
A 300mm (12in) stainless steel type is ideal and can double as a straightedge. For longer measurements a flexible tape type is convenient.

Sliding Square
This is a most convenient type for use on smaller projects, and for checking mitres. It usefully combines the features of try and mitre squares in one precision tool.

Chisels
Three chisels – 6, 12 and 19mm (¼, ½ and ¾in) – form a useful set. The bevelled edge type is generally preferred for fine work.

Gouge
Not often used, but indispensable for some work. A 16mm (⅝in) firmer type is a useful all round size.

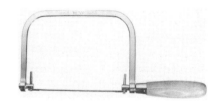

Back Saws
A small dovetail saw 200mm (8in) long, with 20/22 P.P. 25mm (1in), is ideal for much of the fine joint and mitre cutting described in this book. Alternatively, a small tenon saw could be used.

Coping Saw
This is an indispensable tool for all kinds of curved cutting, and its replaceable blade ensures that it can always be in 'as new' cutting condition.

Marking Knife
This is used to make precise lines across the grain when marking joints, and can be used to cut veneers. A hobby type knife can be used instead.

Marking Gauge
This tool is used to mark lines parallel to an edge.

Mortice Gauge
This is a useful, though not essential, tool. Most are equipped with an extra spur for use as a marking gauge.

Jack Plane
This 'jack of all work' is the preferred size for preparing the wood to size for the projects in this book, and for use on the shooting board.

Block Plane
The type shown, with adjustable mouth, is ideal for smoothing the relatively small surfaces involved for the puzzles and games, and for truing mitres on the mitre shooting board.

Rebate Plane
Rebates can usually be cut on a circular saw with rise and fall table, but, without this facility, a rebate plane is essential.

Plough Plane
Grooves can be cut readily with a circular saw, but, otherwise, a plough plane must be used. Metric width blades are more useful than imperial sizes, because the grooves are frequently made to receive plywood and this is always manufactured in metric thicknesses.

Spokeshave
This tool is used for smoothing and chamfering curved edges. The flat sole version is generally more useful than the round sole.

Cabinet Scraper
This simple tool, just a rectangle of thin carbon steel, is useful for cleaning up after planing and for use on veneered surfaces. Its sharpening can be a bit 'hit and miss' until the knack is acquired and, for this reason, it is used less frequently than it deserves.

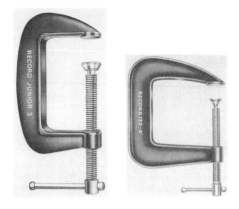

Hand Drill

This tool, often rejected today in favour of the power drill, is nevertheless useful for light hand drilling and countersinking in wood.

Twist Drills

A cased set, ranging from 1.5mm ($\frac{1}{16}$in) to about 8mm ($\frac{5}{16}$in) dia. in 0.5mm ($\frac{1}{32}$in) steps, is ideal, or they can be purchased separately as required. For use mainly with wood, and occasional drilling in metal, the acquisition of carbon steel drills, instead of the high speed steel type (H.S.S.) is a sensible economy.

Forstner Bit

This type of bit, with virtually no point, bores a hole with a smooth base. It is ideal for several of the projects in this book if a special purpose D type bit is not available.

Flat Bits

These inexpensive bits are available in sets, or individually, in a range of sizes from 6mm ($\frac{1}{4}$in) to 38mm ($1\frac{1}{2}$in). They bore quickly and cleanly but it is recommended that they should be used in a pillar drill, where possible, for the projects described in this book.

Countersink Bit

The rose pattern, with parallel shank, is a precision tool and is the preferred type to produce smooth accurate countersinking.

G Cramps

Although pressure can be applied in alternative ways by using some ingenuity together with long bolts or screws and the vice, a selection of G cramps is a very useful addition to the tool kit. One or two of the deep throated type permit

cramping 'well in' from the edge.

Cork Block

Abrasive paper should rarely be applied to wood unless wrapped around a block, and the cork variety offers the best 'feel'.

Abrasive Paper

Not really a tool, but convenient to mention next to the cork block. The 'glass' variety has been superseded by more effective and longer lasting grits including garnet and aluminium oxide, and these should always be used for best results. Coarse grades should not be necessary on this type of work and 120 grit abrasive paper will quickly reduce most wood surfaces to an even, smooth flatness. This can be followed by 180 grit paper to leave the workpiece ready for pre-finishing treatment (raising the grain and/or filling it). A really fine 400 grit 'wet and dry' paper should be used for rubbing down the surface of Rustin's clear plastic coating. A 320 grit garnet paper, or '00' or '000' grade steel wool, is useful for smoothing polished surfaces.

Oilstone

Woodworking in quality hardwoods requires that a keen edge is maintained on all tools. For this purpose a good quality oilstone, either natural or artificial, is essential. The best available is considered to be the Arkansas type, but its high cost will place it beyond the reach of most craftsmen. A fine grade artificial stone, such as India, will produce a good edge quickly and at a reasonable cost. The standard 200 × 50mm (8 × 2in) stone is the preferred size, and it should always be housed in a protective box with a lid. In use the stone should be lubricated with either neatsfoot oil or a light machine type oil.

7

2 WOOD PREPARATION

Preparing the wood for these projects is relatively easy because, usually, quite small sizes are involved. Only one game, Chinese Chequers, is likely to need two or more pieces of wood joined together, edge to edge, to make up the required width. If machine tools are not available to help with the preparation, a rip saw will be useful for dealing with thicker wood. Where possible, board material should be purchased as near as practicable to the finished thickness.

Face Side
One side of the wood should be selected as the face side, then planed flat and true with a jack plane (photo 1). Except on narrow strips of wood, check for flatness by placing the plane sole on edge, across the grain, and view against the light. High spots can then be removed with a few strokes of the plane, then the surface re-tested. The traditional way to test for twist or wind is to use a pair of winding strips, but this is less appropriate in these small sizes. Instead, rest the piece of wood onto a piece of thick glass, or a mirror, and attempt to rock the ends. If rock cannot be induced, the surface is flat; if it can, the diagonally opposite high spots should be noted, then planed away. If the fibres of the wood tear away, the direction of the planing should be reversed to plane with the grain. Interlocking grain will, however, give problems in both directions and can only be scraped or sanded smooth at a later stage. Mark the face side with the usual squiggle ∝.

Face Edge
Next, plane one edge straight and square with the face side. This is usually done with the wood held in the vice but, if difficulty is found in this operation, it can be planed on the shooting board (see chapter 3) provided it is not too long. Mark the face edge with the inverted V mark.

Width
The required *width* can now be set on a marking gauge, then marked from the face edge onto *both* sides of the wood (photo 2). If the wood is only a little oversize it can be planed away; otherwise the excess will have to be sawn off. This can be cut with a band or circular saw, or by hand. When hand sawing, it is often convenient to hold the wood tilted at an angle in the vice (photo 3). Thin wood, in particular, is less likely to split if held in this way. The planing of this edge is easier with the wood held in the vice, because the gauge lines on each side indicate the squareness.

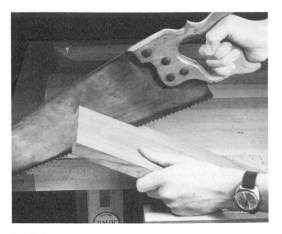

Thickness

Next the wood should be gauged to *thickness*, from the face side, onto both edges. If the wood is wider than about 100mm (4in), it may be helpful to mark the thickness on the end grain also. If a considerable thickness of wood has to be removed it may be easier to use the plane diagonally across the grain. Wood 'peels' away more easily if planed in this direction, and thicker shavings can normally be removed with less effort. Final planing should, or course, be with the grain in the usual way.

Wide Boards

If two or more boards have to be joined together on edge they should each be prepared as described with their face sides held together in the vice with face edges uppermost and in line (photo 4). The edges can now be planed, and any errors of squareness will cancel themselves out when the two boards are placed together side by side. The edges can be glued together under sash cramp pressure (photo 5).

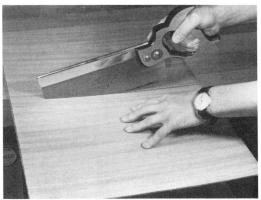

Cutting Plywood

When sawing thin plywood to size it is often convenient to use a back saw, cutting between the jaws of an open vice (photo 6).

3 JIGS AND DEVICES

Cube Sanding Jig

This device enables cubes to be hand-sanded to size, almost as accurately as those produced with the aid of a disc sander. It only takes a little time to make, and even has an advantage over its machine counterpart as two different abrasive surfaces are available for use. One side can be used for rapid truing of the cube and the other, fitted with a really fine abrasive, for finishing. The vee groove size given in the drawing will suit all the cubes used in this book, and can also be used for other end grain truing.

Method

Base board

The base board can be a piece of blockboard, plywood or an off-cut of melamine surfaced chipboard. The latter can usefully reduce the friction of the sanding block as it is moved back and forth.

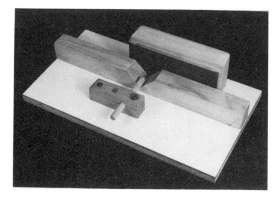

Vee block

The vee block, into which the cubes fit, should be made as accurately as possible by sawing and chiselling out the vee or by the use of a mitre block. To do this, cut the vee block in half lengthwise, saw mitres on the cut ends, then screw the two pieces to the base board in exact alignment. To give working clearance for the abrasive block, a thin strip of wood – 1.5mm

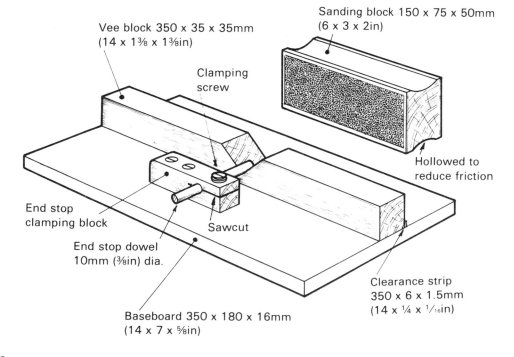

Vee block 350 x 35 x 35mm
(14 x 1⅜ x 1⅜in)

Clamping screw

Sanding block 150 x 75 x 50mm
(6 x 3 x 2in)

Hollowed to reduce friction

End stop clamping block

Sawcut

End stop dowel
10mm (⅜in) dia.

Baseboard 350 x 180 x 16mm
(14 x 7 x ⅝in)

Clearance strip
350 x 6 x 1.5mm
(14 x ¼ x ¹/₁₆in)

($\frac{1}{16}$in) thick – is glued to the lower edge of the vee block, as shown.

End stop

The construction of the simple end stop, easily adjustable to suit different sized cubes, is self explanatory from the drawing. The clamping screw closes the saw cut to grip the dowel firmly.

Sanding block

This should be cut to size and the edges planed accurately square. Friction on the top and bottom edges of the block, which is reversible, can be reduced by chiselling or gouging them slightly hollow. The corners and edges should be rounded to make the block more comfortable to hold. The abrasive paper, with a medium grit on one side and a fine on the other, can be secured to the block with Cow Gum or double-sided adhesive tape. Cow Gum is a very convenient adhesive because, when the abrasive requires renewal, it can be readily peeled off and the residue of gum rubbed away cleanly. If double-sided tape is used it should be applied to cover completely the back of the abrasive, or an uneven surface could result. After sanding with the medium grit abrasive, the stop may require slight forward adjustment to bring the cubes into contact with the finer, and possibly thinner, abrasive side of the block. The friction of the block can be reduced by rubbing a piece of paraffin wax or candle grease onto the base board.

Disc Sander

A disc sander is unequalled for the rapid and accurate truing of cubes, mitres and end grain surfaces generally. The manufactured sander will have a slot machined in the table to receive the guide plate of the adjustable fence, which can be set to any required angle. To produce accurate cubes and rectangular blocks of precise length, a simple jig can be made for use in conjunction with this fence. The jig is a piece of steel or aluminium angle $38 \times 38 \times 5$mm ($1\frac{1}{2} \times 1\frac{1}{2} \times \frac{3}{16}$in), and a little longer than the depth of the table. It can be made from wood, in which case it should be somewhat thicker – 6–8mm ($\frac{1}{4}$–$\frac{5}{16}$in). A stop, of metal or wood, has to be fitted to the inner lower surface of the angle piece, and it is useful if this is slotted to allow different sized pieces of wood to be sanded. If unslotted, it can be fixed into any of its required positions with a small countersunk headed screw and wing nut. Another stop, such as a small machine screw, protrudes from the underside of the angle piece to limit its forward travel to within about 1mm ($\frac{1}{32}$in) of the disc. To adjust the jig, it is held against the fence in its fully forward position against its underside stop. The inner stop is now secured in place with its edge the required cube size from the abrasive disc. In use, a cube of wood is held firmly in position against the stop and into the root of the angle, as the other hand gently feeds the angle forward towards the disc (photo 1). When one side of

the cube has been sanded flat, and *before* the underside stop abuts against the edge of the table, it is turned and another surface sanded, and so on. After initial sanding of *all* the sides, which form an accurate but oversize cube, they can be sanded further until the stop prevents further reduction in size. Note that the finger and thumb pressure, which holds the cube, should be directed at holding it *away* from the disc and tightly against its stop. When sanding rectangular blocks two, three or four cubes, or square pieces, should be used between the inner stop and the disc to give the precise position of the inner stop.

A basic, yet effective, disc sander can easily be made using an old washing machine motor, as shown in photo 2. A table of wood should be arranged to be accurately at right angles to the disc, and about 30mm ($1\frac{1}{4}$in) below its centre

height. A metal sanding disc can be purchased to fit the motor spindle, or a plywood or chipboard disc screwed to a large pulley wheel instead. A 250mm (10in) disc is the ideal size, but a 200mm (8in) one can be used if preferred. If the wooden disc does not revolve truly, it can be corrected by gentle (or heavier!) taps with a hammer against light spots as revealed by a piece of chalk. A 120–150 grit abrasive disc will give a good surface finish to the cube and can be fixed in place with Cow Gum. A block of wood, secured to the table with a small G cramp, can serve as a fence and its 45° or 90° position carefully checked with a combination square.

Mitre Block

A mitre block is often more convenient in use than the generally favoured box variety, because it is easier to judge the position of the saw and also its depth of cut. Its recognised weakness (inaccuracy due to wear in the slots) is minimised in this version by using a generously thick guide block which, by eliminating saw wobble, maintains its precision. Cost apart, a 'home-made' mitre block has the advantage that it can be made to suit the exact width of the kerf made by the dovetail or tenon saw, with which it will be used. However, it is not really practicable to make it without recourse to a circular saw with facilities for cutting mitres, or to a disc sander with mitre fence attachment.

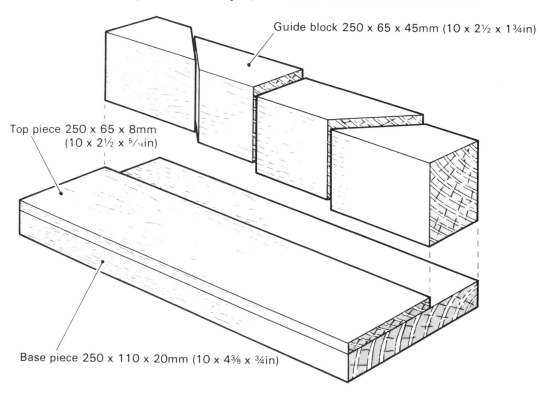

Guide block 250 x 65 x 45mm (10 x 2½ x 1¾in)

Top piece 250 x 65 x 8mm (10 x 2½ x ⁵⁄₁₆in)

Base piece 250 x 110 x 20mm (10 x 4⅜ x ¾in)

Method

Base

The base of the mitre block can be rebated from a solid piece of wood or, as shown in the drawing, made from two pieces glued together. The guide block should be marked out, then sawn off on a circular saw equipped to cut accurate 45° and 90° angles. Alternatively it can be cut by hand or with a bandsaw, then the ends trued to the precise angles with a disc sander. Using either method, the accuracy of the angles should be checked with a combination square and adjustments made as necessary.

Assembly

The four separate blocks now have to be glued and G cramped, or screwed, to the base with just sufficient clearance between them for the saw blade. To ascertain the clearance required, make a saw cut in a piece of wood, across the grain, then insert test pieces of thin card or veneer, or both, into the cut until a good fit is obtained. This can then be used between the blocks to space them as they are secured in

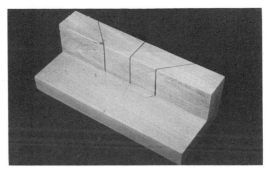

position. This method is likely to be more convenient, and more accurate, than trying to use the saw blade itself to space the blocks apart. Incidentally, if a sharp tenon or dovetail saw does not leave a smooth sawn surface when using the mitre block, it is worthwhile stroking each side of the blade with an oil or slip stone which overlaps the teeth. This will then bring any 'proud' teeth into line and a smoother sawn finish will be obtained. Just one or two strokes with the stone should be sufficient; too enthusiastic use will remove the set on the teeth and cause the blade to bind in its kerf.

Mitre Planing Board

This simple device is well worth making, not only for the projects in this book, but as a permanently useful workshop aid. It enables mitres to be planed easily to a degree of accuracy that would be difficult to equal without recourse to expensive woodworking machinery. It was devised by the author over twenty years ago when it was published in *The Woodworker*, has since appeared in other publications and is now a widely used device. It is particularly useful for truing the mitred corners of the Labyrintspel and Bagatelle games, and can be used for several of the puzzle corner joints, all of which invariably require minute adjustments before a perfect fit can be obtained.

The device can be made full size – for planing carcass boards up to say 500mm (20in) wide and for use with a jack plane – or a compact version as given here. This is used in conjunction with a block plane and is adequate for most other work.

Method

Base board

This should be a piece of blockboard, multi-ply or solid wood and, if possible, the groove should be machined in. If the groove is cut with a plough plane its position should be marked with a cutting or marking gauge first. If it is not possible to machine or plane the groove it can be fabricated by gluing two pieces of 3mm (⅛in) thick plywood to the base with a 3mm (⅛in) gap between them.

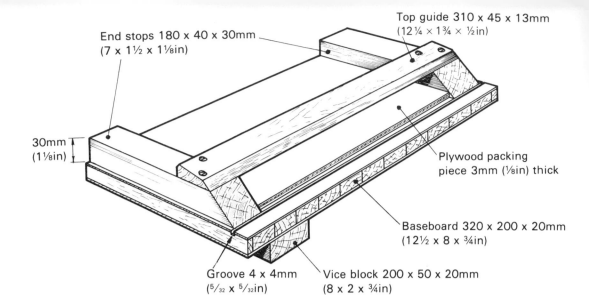

Top guide 310 x 45 x 13mm
(12¼ × 1¾ × ½in)

End stops 180 x 40 x 30mm
(7 x 1½ x 1⅛in)

30mm
(1⅛in)

Plywood packing
piece 3mm (⅛in) thick

Baseboard 320 x 200 x 20mm
(12½ x 8 x ¾in)

Groove 4 x 4mm
($^5/_{32}$ x $^5/_{32}$in)

Vice block 200 x 50 x 20mm
(8 x 2 x ¾in)

End stops
These are blocks of wood with the ends cut accurately to 45°. The mitred ends should be cut on a mitre block then carefully checked with a combination square. The stops are glued and screwed to the base board to be exactly at right angles to the slot and in line with it.

Upper guide
This is a strip of well-seasoned hardwood with one edge bevelled at 45°. Initially it should be pinned in position and only screwed to the end stops when its exact position has been established with the bevelled surfaces exactly aligned.

Packing piece
The base board has to be raised with a piece of 3mm (⅛in) thick plywood to bring the work-piece being planed into the path of the plane blade. This packing piece should fit between the end stops and can be glued and cramped down to the base board or simply pinned to it. Its top edge, adjacent to the groove, should be aligned with the bevelled ends of the stops. A piece of candle or paraffin wax, rubbed along the groove and on the upper guide, will give a smooth and easy sliding action as the plane is used.

Shooting Board

The use of a shooting board enables the end grain of wood parts to be planed accurately square and true. Its use prevents splitting away at the edges, which is always a hazard when planing the end grain. It is also useful when planing veneer edges and squaring the edges of pieces of wood when difficulty is found in doing this in the usual way.

Method
Base board
Any reliable solid wood or manmade board can be used for the base. The shooting board shown in the photograph uses a piece of a melamine

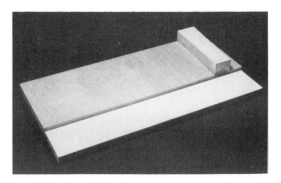

covered kitchen cabinet door with the advantage that the melamine surface reduces friction on the side of the plane.

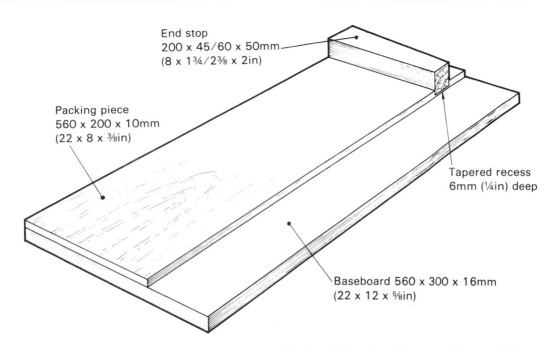

End stop
200 x 45/60 x 50mm
(8 x 1¾/2⅜ x 2in)

Packing piece
560 x 200 x 10mm
(22 x 8 x ⅜in)

Tapered recess
6mm (¼in) deep

Baseboard 560 x 300 x 16mm
(22 x 12 x ⅝in)

Packing piece

The packing piece is necessary to give a rebate for the plane to work against and to raise the wood being planed into the path of the plane blade. A small chamfer, planed on the lower edge of the packing piece, will reduce friction with the corner of the plane and prevent a build up of dust becoming a nuisance here.

End stop

The recess for this can be tapered as shown which usefully allows the stop to be tapped into place to give a tight fit. Another advantage is that if the square end of the stop becomes damaged through wear, or if the plane is allowed to tilt, a few shavings taken off the tapered back edge of the stop will allow it to move forward, and another square end can then be cut. To allow for subsequent adjustments, the stop should be screwed in place from the underside.

Veneering Press

It is suggested that the larger board games, with veneered playing surfaces, should have these glued down under pressure using a caul and bearer press. Other methods can be used for general veneering, but when somewhat intricate 'made up' surfaces are involved it is the most reliable technique to adopt.

Method

Bearers

The sizes given for the top and bottom bearers may be varied to suit the available wood which can, of course, be old or secondhand. The upper bearers are curved and made smaller than the lower ones which have to remain straight

under tension. The cross section of the lower bearers should be about twice that of the upper ones. Sufficient bearers are required to apply pressure about every 100mm (4in) along the

15

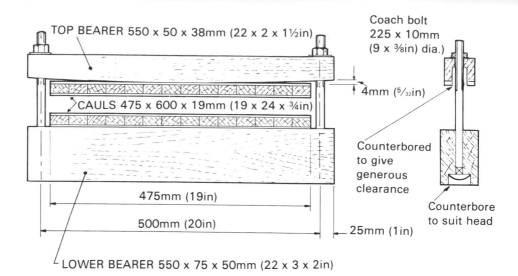

TOP BEARER 550 x 50 x 38mm (22 x 2 x 1½in)

Coach bolt
225 x 10mm
(9 x ⅜in) dia.)

CAULS 475 x 600 x 19mm (19 x 24 x ¾in)

4mm (5/32in)

Counterbored
to give
generous
clearance

Counterbore
to suit head

475mm (19in)

500mm (20in)

25mm (1in)

LOWER BEARER 550 x 75 x 50mm (22 x 3 x 2in)

panel being veneered. However, if sufficient G cramps are available, the end bearers can be dispensed with, and the cramps used to provide pressure at the ends. Using about eight cramps, only three pairs of bearers are necessary to veneer the largest board game surface (Chess) given in this book.

Some of the waste to be removed in forming the curved lower edge of the first top bearer can be cut away with a band or circular saw although in practice it is but a few minutes work to plane the curve to shape. After planing, hold a thin lathe of wood in contact with the curve, to reveal any flats or high spots which should then be removed. Check the bearer further by clamping it down to a flat surface, noting any gaps and inaccuracies in the line of contact. When a fair curve has been obtained it can be sanded, then used as a template for the other top battens which can be shaped and checked as described.

A bench or pillar type drill should be used, if possible, for drilling the bolt holes to ensure their squareness and accurate alignment. Note that the holes in the top bearers are drilled clearance size and counterbored. This counterbore permits uneven tightening of the bearers, without binding, which expedites the procedure. It is worthwhile recessing the bolt heads into the lower bearers to give a smooth under surface. This can be done with a flat bit before the bolt holes are drilled.

Bolts
Coach bolts have a short square section under the head which will prevent them turning as

they are tightened, and are the obvious choice if available. Some counterboring of the hole may be necessary to receive the square section, because the holes are close to the bearer ends and the usual driving in of the bolts may split them. If machine bolts are used instead of the preferred coach bolts, the recesses for the heads can be drilled a little undersize and the hexagonal heads driven in flush to prevent them turning.

Cauls
The cauls can be pieces of better quality chipboard at least 16mm (⅝in) thick or, preferably, blockboard or multi-ply. For economy it is possible to dispense with the lower caul, and place the groundwork being veneered directly on the lower bearers. This should prove satisfactory provided the groundwork is at least 16mm (⅝in) thick.

Using the press
Speed is essential when closing down the press and the rapid tightening of the nuts is greatly facilitated by using a socket set ratchet wrench. Alternatively a box spanner may be used, but it is unlikely that an open ended spanner can be manipulated quickly enough to provide the necessary pressure before the glue starts to gel.

Few problems are usually encountered when using a press for veneering, but one that should be avoided is overtightening of the nuts. This can actually *reduce* pressure in the centre of the caul, particularly if the groundwork being veneered is narrower than the maximum width the press will accept. It is prudent to use a

16

straightedge, adjacent to each top bearer, when tightening the nuts, to check that the top caul remains truly flat.

Glues

Two main types of glue are readily available for woodworking use and both can give excellent results in a veneer press. They are the popular 'white' PVA adhesive, and the long established water resistant synthetic resin (Cascamite, Aerolite) type. The PVA type tends to have a shorter 'working' life than the other and this may dictate the choice. If the total time required to spread the glue, position and secure the veneer, and tighten down the press is longer than about seven minutes, it may be better to use the resin type glue. Because it is impossible to give a 'working' time for adhesives – this is dependent not only on the formula of the glue but also on the ambient temperature – a simple test can give the answer. Spread a thin layer of PVA glue onto a piece of wood and check the time that elapses before it changes its consistency. If it does not change significantly in the time it would take to complete the veneering it is safe to use. Otherwise the slower setting synthetic resin glue could be the better choice but a test is also recommended.

4 FINISHING

Four finishes have been used on the puzzles and games presented in this book and each has particular, though not exclusive, advantages in specific instances. They are white or transparent French (shellac) polish, polyurethane seal or varnish, Danish oil (an improvement on the once popular teak oil) and Clear Plastic Coating (Rustin's). Each will be dealt with generally, and, at the end of the chapter, one or more of these finishes is suggested for the various parts of the puzzles and games.

French Polish

In most cases here it is used as a brush polish, and not bodied up with a rubber in the traditional way, to produce the familiar high gloss finish. It is less popular than formerly as other finishes have supplanted it, except in restoration work. Its advantages are its very rapid drying action, its preservation of the true colour of the wood and the fact that several coats can be applied without building up a surface thickness which could interfere, unduly, with the assembly of puzzle pieces.

The polish should be applied with a soft brush or mop and left to dry for fifteen minutes or so. The surfaces can then be smoothed lightly, with 000 grade steel wool, before further coats are applied. Each coat, including the last, should be smoothed lightly, then a little wax polish rubbed on to produce an attractive dull sheen. This is not a particularly hardwearing finish but is very easy to apply, and further coats can be applied with minimum delay. It reacts favourably with rub-down letters, and can be used to seal them in locally to protect them against more aggressive finishes. It can be used, on a folded pad of cloth, to polish turned pieces – or men – revolving in the lathe or in a drill chuck. The pad should not be saturated with polish, but replenished with very small quantities from time to time. Just a touch of linseed oil on the pad will lubricate it, and prevent it sticking, during this operation.

Danish Oil

This is the easiest finish to apply – it is simply rubbed into the surface of the wood with a piece of cloth. It penetrates and seals the wood without leaving a surface film. It dries in four to six hours, depending on temperature and humidity, and may then be re-coated. When dry, its low lustre appearance can be improved by rubbing with a soft cloth. Its resistance to chipping and scratching makes it ideal for puzzles with individual pieces that are frequently assembled and dismantled, and where an unobtrusive finish is acceptable. If used over rub-down letters or numbers, these should first be sealed in with a coat or two of French (shellac) polish.

Polyurethane Varnish

This is perhaps the most popular wood finish today and is available in gloss, satin and matt. It is easy to apply by brush, and dries to a hardwearing chip-free surface. It has considerable 'body' and is therefore unsuitable for puzzle parts which have to fit together closely. Its particular use is for the carcase and base parts of puzzles and games and, for these, the matt or satin finishes would generally be preferred.

Apply the varnish evenly to the surface, with a suitable paint brush, then leave to dry in a warm, dust free atmosphere for eight to twelve hours. The first and second coats should be smoothed lightly, with a fine abrasive paper, and wiped clean before the final coat is applied.

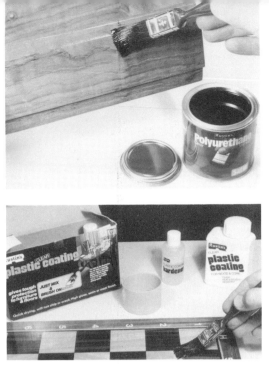

Clear Plastic Coating (Rustin's)

This clear finish, a compound of butylated urea-formaldehyde, plasticised with alkyd and reinforced with melamine, is ideal for the playing decks of games, particularly those on which steel balls run. It can be given a satin finish, if preferred, or rubbed down and burnished to a high gloss mirror-like surface which is extremely hardwearing and also both heat and solvent resistant. Details for applying this two-part finish, which is brushed on, are supplied with the pack.

Surface Pre-Treatment

Many wood finishes raise the grain slightly when they are applied and this means that extra smoothing, to the first coat at least, will be necessary. For this reason, it is usually preferable to raise the grain deliberately by rubbing the workpiece over with a damp cloth first and then, when dry, smoothing it with a fine grit abrasive. This gives a tangible improvement to the feel of the surface, and it is recommended that this should always be done before the first coat of finish is applied. Loose dust can be wiped away with a cloth lightly dampened with methylated spirits (wood alcohol).

Grain Filling

Some species of wood (sycamore, beech and yew, for example) are close grained and filling is quite unnecessary, but, for other open grained varieties, filling the grain before applying the finish can be worthwhile. The instructions with the wood finish should be consulted first, because certain fillers and finishes are incompatible.

Under Surfaces

For best heirloom quality it is recommended that, where appropriate, the under surfaces of the puzzles and games should be covered with baize. If offcuts of the billiard table variety are available (see Yellow Pages for refurbishing specialists) this would be ideal. Its heavy quality resists glue penetration, and its weave is

such that it does not fray easily.

It can be secured in place with woodworking PVA glue or an impact adhesive. When fitting baize into the recessed underside of puzzles it is often convenient to cut out a paper or thin card template to size first. This can then be placed over the baize and cut round with a knife and straightedge. When fitted to flat undersides, the baize should be glued on oversize initially then trimmed round with a sharp knife when the adhesive is dry.

It is a nice touch to sign and date work of which you are proud, and this looks well if done inside a circle cut in the baize. A piece of sharpened tube, of suitable size, can be used to cut out the circle and, even if its edge is not particularly sharp, will work well if used onto the *end* grain of the block of wood.

Small discs of baize, filled into the sockets and recesses of the puzzles and games, can enhance their appearance. These can be cut out, as described, using a sharpened piece of tube and, if double-sided tape is fixed to the strip of baize first, the fiddly operation of gluing them into place will be avoided.

Suitable Finishes

	Puzzles	French Polish	Danish Oil	Polyurethane	Plastic Coating
1	Black to White				
	Tray	•		•	
	Blocks	•	•		
2	Board Puzzle				
	Board			•	
	Pieces	•	•		
3	Boat Puzzle				
	Board	•		•	
	Men	•			
4	Chinese Cube				
	Pieces	•	•		
	Base			•	
5	Easy Cube				
	Pieces	•	•		
	Base			•	
6	Five into One Square				
	Pieces	•	•	•	
	Holder	•	•		
7	Magic Square				
	Pegs	•			
	Base	•		•	
8	Puzzle Cubes				
	Cubes	•	•	•	•
	Holder	•		•	
9	Number Sequence				
	Blocks	•	•		
	Tray	•		•	
10	Six Piece Chinese Puzzle	•	•		
11	Steady Hand Puzzle	•		•	•
12	Three Piece Chinese Puzzle	•	•		
13	Tower of Hanoi				
	Base	•		•	•
	Discs	•	•		
14	Travel Solitaire	•		•	•
15	Tricky Hook	•			

	Games	French Polish	Danish Oil	Polyurethane	Plastic Coating
1	Bagatelle				
	Case			•	
	Playing deck				•
	Other parts	•		•	
2	Chess Board			•	•
3	Chinese Chequers			•	•
4	Labyrintspel				
	Carcase and frames			•	
	Playing deck	•			•
	Barriers	•		•	
5	Nine Men's Morris			•	•
6	Noughts and Crosses	•	•		

5
PUZZLES

1 Black to White

With this intriguing little puzzle you can compete with yourself, or with friends, in attempting to reverse the positions of the words BLACK and WHITE. It is not too frustrating as most puzzlers can effect the transposition given unlimited time, but the skill lies in doing it in as few moves, or as quickly as possible. Perhaps because it uses words its appeal is wider than usual, and even extends to those whose interest in puzzles is less than compulsive. It is a worthwhile project to make, both for the satisfyingly smooth sliding action of the cubes and for its smart functional appearance.

Object
This is explained by the title and has been covered by the introduction. It is simply to reverse the positions of the words by manoeuvring the letter cubes inside the tray.

Construction
Quite challenging to make with hand tools alone, but, conversely, easy and straightforward with mechanical aids to shape the letter blocks accurately, and to true the mitred corners of the tray.

Materials
The puzzle shown is made of Brazilian tulip wood with cubes of sycamore. The silky white surface of the sycamore is an excellent one on which to fix the letters to give them maximum contrast and clarity. The relatively rare tulip wood makes a most attractive tray for the cubes, and together they provide a delightful combination.

Many hardwoods are suitable for this project but that selected for the letter blocks should be as close grained as possible to give a suitable surface for the rub-down letters. Dark wood blocks can have white or gold letters affixed to give good contrast.

Prepared sizes

Cubes (12)	300 × 20mm (12 × ¾in) square
Sides	400 × 20 × 6mm (16 × ¾ × ¼in)
Base	105 × 66 × 6mm (4¼ × 2½ × ¼in)
Baize for base	
Rub-down letters	12mm (½in) high

Method

Cubes
The letter blocks should be made first, then the tray made to fit them. Traditionally the blocks are cubes – as in the version shown here – but lower blocks will probably have a better sliding action. They are less likely to tilt as finger pressure is used to slide them, and are more tolerant of slight inaccuracies in size.

Prepare a length of wood accurately square – or rectangular, if lower blocks are preferred – and long enough to allow a few spare pieces to be made. It is not necessary to mark them off to length if they are cut with the aid of a mitre block or a circular saw. If using a mitre block, clamp or nail a stop to it to allow the pieces to be sawn off to the required length. Check the first piece sawn off – it should be the same length as the width of the wood. Saw off at least twelve pieces (photo 1).

1. Sawing the letter blocks to length

All the sides of the blocks can be finished to the correct size with the aid of a disc sander or by using a cube sanding jig (photo 2). See chapter 3. The exact size of the blocks is not critical but uniformity is or the blocks will not slide smoothly past each other. When they are

2. Sanding the letter blocks square and to size

completed they should be further smoothed by rubbing onto a sheet of fine abrasive paper pinned, or fixed with double-sided adhesive tape, to a flat piece of wood. Aim to draw each side of each block two or three times along the abrasive, going with the grain where appropriate. Next, slightly chamfer or round all edges

in a similar way, by turning the block with the fingers and thumb as the edges are drawn along it.

Tray

The material for the sides and ends of the tray should be prepared to the sizes given, but can be somewhat narrower if lower, non-cuboid blocks are used. One edge can be rebated to receive the base but, if preferred, this can be omitted. To ascertain the precise size of the tray, five letter blocks should be held together with an elastic band and the overall length measured (photo 3). Also check the length of

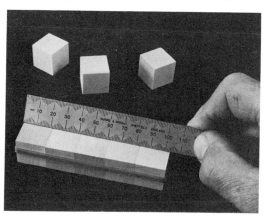

3. Measuring the length of five cubes

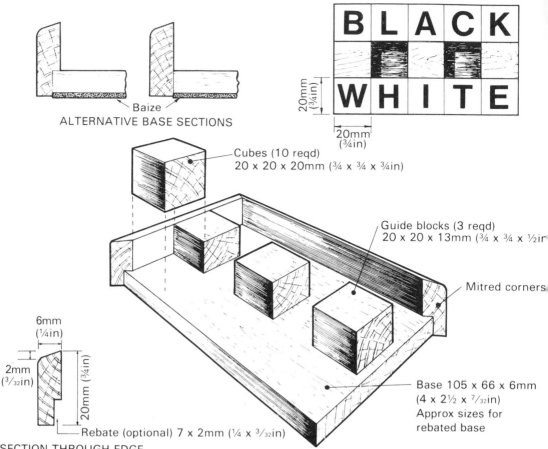

ALTERNATIVE BASE SECTIONS

Baize

BLACK WHITE

20mm (¾in)

20mm (¾in)

Cubes (10 reqd)
20 x 20 x 20mm (¾ x ¾ x ¾in)

Guide blocks (3 reqd)
20 x 20 x 13mm (¾ x ¾ x ½in)

Mitred corners

Base 105 x 66 x 6mm
(4 x 2½ x ⁷/₃₂in)
Approx sizes for
rebated base

6mm (¼in)

2mm (³/₃₂in)

20mm (¾in)

Rebate (optional) 7 x 2mm (¼ x ³/₃₂in)

SECTION THROUGH EDGE

three blocks to give the width of the tray. Transfer these sizes onto the edge material and cut the mitred ends slightly overlong with a fine toothed tenon or dovetail saw.

The ends can now be trued accurately to length with the aid of a mitre planing jig (photo

4. Planing the mitred ends of the tray sides

4). See chapter 3. Hold the corners of the tray together with sellotape and test the fit of the cubes inside it. It should be such that a very slightly loose sliding action is obtained. This, after polishing, should remove the clearance and give a near perfect action.

Apply two extra layers of sellotape to the outside of the edges then apply glue to the mitres (photo 5). The tray can now be hinged together, joined with more tape and excess glue removed with a damp cloth. Check for squareness before setting aside to dry.

Fit the base before removing the tape from the edges. If the edges are rebated, the thickness of the base should be such that a small recess is formed on the underside to receive the baize. The same effect can be obtained with non-rebated edges by pressing the base slightly upwards when it is glued into place (photo 6). When dry, plane the slight bevel on the top edges of the tray and smooth all surfaces with a fine abrasive, used on a sanding block.

24

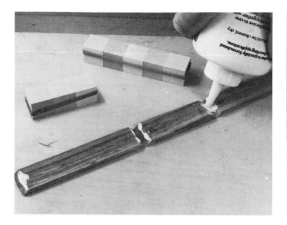

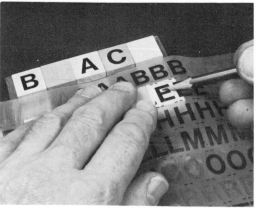

5. Gluing the tray sides

7. Applying the rub-down letters

Next prepare the three guide blocks which are glued in the tray. These should normally be of the same wood species as that used for the tray edges. They are made in the same way as the letter blocks, but, in height, should be flush with the tray edges. To locate these blocks it is necessary to assemble the letter blocks in the tray also. A few minutes after gluing the guide blocks in place, the letter blocks should be removed to avoid the possibility of glue adhering to them.

6. Gluing on the base

Finishing

This, and the fixing of the baize to the underside, is dealt with in chapter 4. However, some finishing details, peculiar to the letter blocks, are offered here. A quick and reliable finish (one that does not build up an undue thickness that could give problems) is white or transparent French polish (shellac). Each block should have two sealing coats of polish applied with a soft brush. Next they should be rubbed onto a piece of well-worn fine abrasive (350–400 grit) pinned flat to a piece of wood. The rub-down letters can most easily be applied with the blocks in the tray, as the adjacent ones help to keep the backing sheet flat and cockle free (photo 7). Two or three further coats of French polish, the last rubbed down as before, will give smoothly sliding and well finished blocks. Finally, a little wax polish rubbed on will complete the cubes. Two appealing features of French polish are its rapid drying action – in a warm atmosphere it can receive another coat in ten minutes – and its ability to cover rub-down letters without inter-action.

2 Board Puzzle

Devotees of jigsaw puzzles will find this an interesting variation on which to test their patience and skill, and could well be surprised at their own performance. It is a considerable test of spatial perception and, although more than one solution is possible, many will find that it will defeat them. Some are slow to acknowledge this. The puzzle often appears to be almost solved, and tempts the puzzler again to try slight re-arrangements.

The use of contrasting woods, interlocking into parquetry like patterns and contained within a polished hardwood frame, creates an attractive puzzle that rarely fails to arouse interest. To enable the pieces to be handled more easily without introducing unsightly clearance between them, they are made thicker than the centre cross and the surrounding frame.

Object
To fit all the pieces into the frame. This can be achieved in two ways; haphazardly or with the pieces arranged to give a symmetrically multi-banded pattern.

Construction
Not easy; particularly the fitting of mitred corners of the frame. Long mitred corners such as these are notoriously difficult to 'get right', but the clamping jig detailed is a considerable help in overcoming the problems. This apart, the construction should not present any problems, particularly if the blocks can be jig sanded to size.

Materials
The puzzle shown is made with the frame and centre cross of figured teak with sycamore, Indian rosewood, yew and padauk pieces. These rest on a plywood base covered in green baize. Almost any contrasting well-seasoned offcuts of hardwood could be utilised for this puzzle.

Prepared sizes

Frame	970 × 50 × 10mm (38 × 2 × ⅜in)
Cross	65 × 65 × 5mm (2½ × 2½ × 3/16in)
Base	270 × 180 × 3mm (10½ × 7 × ⅛in) plywood
Gusset	120 × 60 × 4mm (4¾ × 2⅜ × 5/32in) plywood
Pieces	
Each band (3 required of different woods)	450 × 20 × 10mm (18 × ¾ × ⅜in)
Squares	150 × 20 × 10mm (6 × ¾ × ⅜in)

Baize required for both sides of base

Method

Because it is difficult to anticipate the final overall size of the pieces, they should be made first and the frame then made to fit them.

Puzzle pieces
The individual blocks, which are glued together to form the pieces, are either one, two, three or four squares long. The recommended procedure, therefore, is to shape the squares accurately to size first, then cut and true the rectangular blocks to be multiples of the squares. The different wood species should each be prepared accurately parallel and to the

1. Gluing the blocks together

glue removed, by rubbing them against a sheet of fine abrasive paper fixed down to a board. A final smoothing of all edges and ends, with fine steel wool, will complete the blocks ready for finishing.

Frame
The width and depth of the rebate can be marked on the prepared wood with a marking gauge. It can be cut most readily with a circular saw or planer, or by hand using a rebate plane (photo 2). Extreme accuracy is not essential in jointing the frame, except to get well fitted mitres, because the precise internal shape of the frame will be marked on at a later stage using a template. The internal length and width of the frame, at this stage, is given by the length of nine and five squares respectively (photo 3),

same width and thickness. The squares can be sawn off on a mitre block to be just slightly longer than they are wide. The sawn ends can most easily be made square and precisely the right length with the aid of a disc sander used with a jig, or by hand with a cube sanding jig (see chapter 3). When the squares have been made, assemblies of two, three or four can be sellotaped together to give the lengths of the rectangular blocks. These can then be sawn off, and their ends sanded until they are identical in length with the test blocks, which have been taped together. By reference to the drawing, the individual blocks can be arranged as shown, then sellotaped into position on one side. A little glue can now be introduced between the blocks by hinging them apart (photo 1). Further sellotape can be bound round to hold the blocks in good contact with each other, or they can be held by light G cramp pressure. Where possible, excess glue should be removed with a damp cloth before setting the pieces aside to dry. The surfaces can be made flat, and traces of

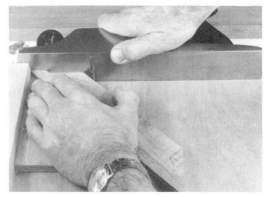

3. Measuring the combined length of the pieces

and this size is transferred onto the inner rebated edges. The mitres should be sawn, just clear of the marked lengths, on a mitre block. Their ends can be trued on a disc sander with mitre fence attachment, or by planing on a shooting board. To adapt the board for this purpose, a triangle of wood, accurately

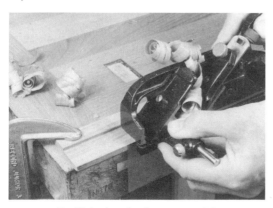

2. Rebating the frame material

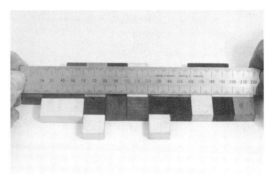

4. Planing the mitred ends of the frame material

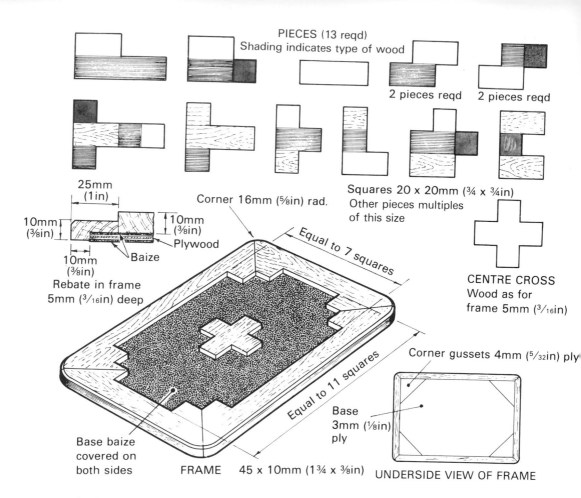

PIECES (13 reqd)
Shading indicates type of wood

2 pieces reqd   2 pieces reqd

25mm (1in)

10mm (³⁄₈in)

10mm (³⁄₈in)
Plywood
Baize

10mm (³⁄₈in)

Rebate in frame
5mm (³⁄₁₆in) deep

Corner 16mm (⅝in) rad.

Squares 20 x 20mm (¾ x ¾in)
Other pieces multiples
of this size

CENTRE CROSS
Wood as for
frame 5mm (³⁄₁₆in)

Equal to 7 squares

Equal to 11 squares

Corner gussets 4mm (⁵⁄₃₂in) ply

Base
3mm (⅛in)
ply

Base baize
covered on
both sides

FRAME   45 x 10mm (1¾ x ⅜in)

UNDERSIDE VIEW OF FRAME

prepared with two edges at 45°, should be nailed in place (photo 4). When planing the opposite end mitre to that shown a piece of wood, the same thickness as the depth of the rebate, should be placed in the rebate to prevent the frame wood from tilting. When two mitred ends have been planed they should be held in

5. Gluing the frame together in the clamping jig

good contact and their squareness checked. Any error detected should be corrected by slight adjustment to the 45° triangular block.

This type of frame, with wide mitred corners, is not easy to hold together either when checking the fit of the corners or when gluing it together. To overcome this difficulty it is well worth making a simple jig to help with both operations. This is a rectangle of chipboard or plywood, with holes drilled near the corners to receive short pieces of dowel (photo 5). Pressure on the mitres is provided by small wedges tapped in place between the dowels and the edge of the frame. Because the internal size of the frame is *not* critical, considerable adjustment can be made to the mitres until satisfactory joints are obtained.

Corner gussets
The stepped corners, and the rebated section of the frame, conveniently allow plywood triangular gusset pieces to be glued into the

6. Gluing the plywood gussets into place

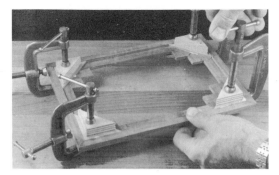

8. Using a coping saw to cut the internal shape

corners to strengthen the relatively weak mitred joints. The plywood for these should be thinner than the depth of the rebate, to give a recess on the underside into which the baize can be fitted. Small blocks of wood are necessary under the G cramps on each side of the workpiece (photo 6). This photograph shows the corners being glued *after* the internal edges of the frame have been shaped. Hindsight suggests that the corners should be strengthened first!

7. Using a template to mark the internal shape of the frame

Internal shaping

The overall internal size of the frame – eleven squares long by seven squares wide – should be accurately marked on to a piece of card and the corners cut out equal in size to three squares. This template can now be placed over the frame and its outline marked on with pencil. Check that the mitres are aligned with the corner cut outs (photo 7). Much of the waste wood from the frame can be removed with a coping saw (photo 8), then the internal edges trued up by careful chiselling and the use of a sharp smooth cut file. The external corners can be rounded,

then a small chamfer worked on the outer frame edge with a block plane.

Base

This is a rectangle of thin plywood, with the corners cut away, which fits into the frame rebate. It should be made to be a good fit because only its edges are effectively glued to the frame. The baize which covers it should be glued on oversize, then trimmed round with a knife when the glue is dry. Later, when the frame has been polished, it can be glued and cramped into place.

Cross

This part, which permits easier lifting and adjustment of the pieces, is cut to the size of five squares from a piece of the frame wood. A file is useful when truing the internal corners of the cross accurately square. Glued to the underside of the cross is a smaller thinner one which fits through the baize lining and is glued to the base. The pieces should be fitted into the frame around the cross when locating its position. The baize can be cut out with a marking knife then the cross glued in place (photo 9).

Finishing

This is dealt with generally in chapter 4.

9. Gluing the cross in position

3 Boat Puzzle

This unusual and interesting puzzle is undeservedly less well known than many presented in this book. It was registered in London in 1842–3 by Jaques & Son of Hatton Garden, who were well known manufacturers of games involving turnery. In its original form, an example of which is in the Pinto collection of Treen in the City of Birmingham Museum, the puzzle consists of a flat board with inlaid lines to represent the river banks. This version has raised banks to give a three-dimensional effect, and to provide secure sockets for the gentlemen and their slaves. It is not an easy puzzle to solve, and can therefore be guaranteed to give hours of fun and mystification. It is an appealing puzzle visually and, with a 'working' model boat which sails across the river from bank to bank, has a fascinating action that will delight puzzlers of all ages. An amusing variation of the puzzle consists of jealous husbands whose wives must not be left on either bank unless accompanied by their respective husbands!

Object

As originally printed in 1840:

'Three gentlemen with their three black slaves desired to cross the river, but as they would have been overpowered and killed by the blacks if they had allowed the latter to exceed them in number on either side of the river (whether in or out of the boat), they contrived to cross in such a way that the gentlemen were always in excess, or at least equal in number to the slaves. The difficulty of the gentlemen was increased by the circumstance of only two of the party, viz. one slave and one gentleman being able to row; one rower or both had therefore always to accompany the boat in its passage to and fro. The white pieces represent the gentlemen, the black their slaves; those who can row being indicated by dots on their heads.'

Construction

Easy. There is little about the puzzle that requires much accuracy in construction, and it is well suited to the woodworker with little experience. It can be made even easier by omitting the rebated river banks and gluing them directly down on to a wider 'river'.

Materials

The river of the puzzle shown here is made of Rio rosewood, a beautiful, once popular timber, now relatively rare because of its cost. The river banks are of padauk and the boat of cocobola. The slaves are of ebony, the gentlemen of Lignum Vitae sapwood, and the boat-securing button of boxwood.

Prepared sizes

River	260 × 120 × 4mm
	(10 × 4¾ × ⁵⁄₃₂in)
Banks	280 × 28 × 21mm (10¾ × 1⅛ × ¹³⁄₁₆in)
Boat	60 × 25 × 14mm (2⅜ × 1 × ⁹⁄₁₆in)
Boat button	50 × 25mm (2 × 1in) square
Gentlemen (light coloured wood)	150 × 16mm (6 × ⅝in) square
Slaves (dark coloured wood)	150 × 16mm (6 × ⅝in) square
Base cover	120 × 40 × 0.5mm (4¾ × 1½ × ¹⁄₃₂in) veneer or thin plywood

Baize for base and to line sockets

Method

'River' or base

This is made from two layers of thin wood, glued together at right angles to give the necessary strength. Because it is unlikely that thin wood will be available in the required width, two or more pieces will require gluing together edge to edge to make the top layer. Their edges can be planed on a shooting board (see chapter 3) until a good fit between them is obtained. Sash cramps or vice pressure can be used to hold the edges in close contact during the gluing operation. A piece of wood under the 'river', and blocks G cramped above it, will prevent any buckling of the thin wood as the vice pressure is applied (photo 1). Paper must

be used over the joints to prevent exuding glue causing problems. When dry, the jointed wood should be planed or scraped flat and true on both sides. After planing to the finished width, a centre line can be marked across its width to give the slot position. The end holes, which give the length of the slot, can now be marked and drilled. The width of the slot is cut in with a marking knife, aligning the blade of the square with the outer edges of the holes at each end. Most of the slot waste can be sawn away with a coping or fret saw (photo 2). A sharp file is a useful tool when cleaning out the slot and, if the wood is hard and brittle, is likely to be more effective than a chisel (photo 3).

The lower layer of the top is in two halves, and the gap between them accommodates the head of the turned button which anchors the boat to the river. This gap is covered by a piece of veneer, or thin aero-modeller's plywood, to give a flat under-surface on which to fix the baize. To receive this covering piece, both inner

edges of the lower layer must be rebated to its thickness. This can be done with a rebate plane or, if the extent of the rebate is marked with a gauge, it could be chiselled to shape instead. The two pieces can now be glued and G cramped into place under the top layer, with each set back 8mm ($^5/_{16}$in) either side of the slot. When dry the river can be sawn to length and the ends trued on a shooting board (see chapter 3).

River banks
These are rebated on their lower edges to receive the thickness of the river. Unless done by machine, it is usually more convenient to rebate overwide or over-thick wood, as shown in photo 4. Here a short piece of wood is being rebated on each side before being sawn to width and thickness. Alternatively, if the wood is prepared to the finished section, but extra long, it can be screwed through its ends on to a block of wood which can be gripped in the vice. Both edges of the river banks are planed to a slight angle, but the size of this should not be gauged on the outside edge as the spur mark will show. The banks should be glued to the river overlong

2. Sawing the slot in the base

1. Gluing the base pieces together

3. Smoothing the slot with a file

31

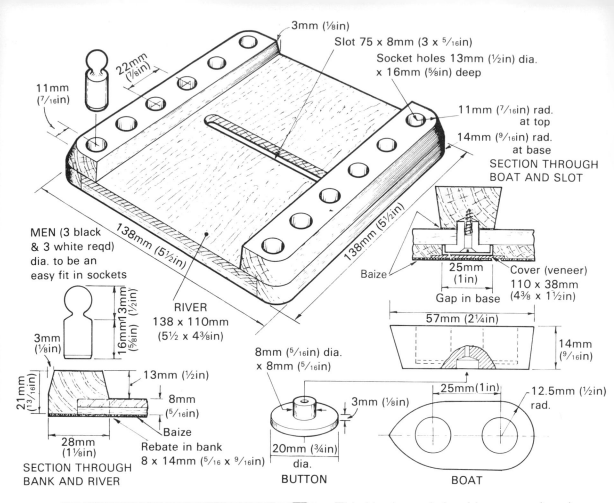

3mm (⅛in)

Slot 75 x 8mm (3 x ⁵⁄₁₆in)

Socket holes 13mm (½in) dia.
x 16mm (⅝in) deep

22mm
(⅞in)

11mm
(⁷⁄₁₆in)

11mm (⁷⁄₁₆in) rad.
at top

14mm (⁹⁄₁₆in) rad.
at base

SECTION THROUGH
BOAT AND SLOT

MEN (3 black
& 3 white reqd)
dia. to be an
easy fit in sockets

138mm (5½in)

138mm (5½in)

Baize

25mm
(1in)

Cover (veneer)
110 x 38mm
(4⅜ x 1½in)

Gap in base

RIVER
138 x 110mm
(5½ x 4⅜in)

16mm 13mm
(⅝in) (½in)

3mm
(⅛in)

8mm (⁵⁄₁₆in) dia.
x 8mm (⁵⁄₁₆in)

57mm (2¼in)

14mm
(⁹⁄₁₆in)

21mm
(1³⁄₁₆in)

13mm (½in)

8mm
(⁵⁄₁₆in)

3mm (⅛in)

25mm(1in)

12.5mm (½in)
rad.

Baize

28mm
(1⅛in)

Rebate in bank
8 x 14mm (⁵⁄₁₆ x ⁹⁄₁₆in)

20mm (¾in)
dia.

SECTION THROUGH
BANK AND RIVER

BUTTON

BOAT

4. Rebating the river banks

then cut to length and shaped later. A block plane is useful when trimming the end grain of the banks to the same angle as the sides, and a spokeshave will deal with the rounded corners.

Sockets
The positions of these can be marked on the banks then drilled with a flat bit, if available.

This bit gives a hole with a square base into which it is easy to fit discs of baize. Set the depth stop to limit the depth of the sockets to 16mm (⅝in). If the drilling can be done with a pillar drill, holes accurately square with the surface will be made.

Boat
The shape of this, and its socket centres, can be marked onto a card template, or, if preferred, directly onto the wood. The sockets are drilled as deep as possible without penetrating the lower surface, and a shallow hole is drilled in the underside to receive the button spigot. The boat can be shaped by chiselling (photo 5), or sawn out with a bandsaw. The edges can be spokeshaved smooth, then finished with fine abrasive paper wrapped over a block.

Boat-anchoring button
A really dense hardwood should be used for this if it is to be turned to shape. This can be done

5. Paring the sides of the boat

with an improvised lathe 'set up', as described below for turning the men, using a chisel to reduce the diameter of the spigot until it is a good fit in the boat. It can be sawn to length, and a small hole drilled and countersunk in the centre to receive the fixing screw. Alternatively, to avoid turning the button, it could be fabricated from a disc of plywood glued to a piece of dowel.

Men

Six of these are required; three black and three white. One of each colour is identified as a rower by an opposite coloured 'dot' on its head. They require turning to shape and this can be

6. Turning the men to shape

done, if a lathe is not available, using an electric drill on a stand and with a wooden tool rest. Wood for the men can be chiselled roughly round at one end for gripping in the chuck, then turned to shape, as shown, with a chisel (photo 6). A triangular file is useful for shaping the neck, and a good finish can quite soon be

obtained with a strip of fine abrasive. Before sawing the men off to length – this can be done as they rotate – a small taper should be cut at their 'feet' end to allow easier entry into their sockets. As they rotate, one man of each colour should have a hole drilled in his head by holding a drill firmly against it. Slight wobbling of the drill, which may cause the hole to enlarge, is of little consequence as the small round pieces of wood which fit can be made slightly tapered when they are turned. The identifying 'dots' can be glued in place, then sawn off and smoothed to the contours of the 'cranium'.

Finishing

This is dealt with generally in chapter 4. After polishing, a piece of baize should be glued to the bottom of the boat to give it a smooth, quiet action as it crosses the river. When the button has been screwed to the boat, the base cover can be fixed in place with two narrow strips of double-sided adhesive tape. This will allow the cover to be pulled away at a later date, if attention is ever needed. Finally the base can be covered with baize, and small discs of the same material used to line the bottoms of the sockets. If double-sided adhesive tape is secured to a strip of baize, discs can be readily punched out with a sharpened piece of tube (photo 7). This should be done over the *end* grain of a block of wood and, after removing the backing paper from the adhesive surface, the discs are immediately ready for pressing into place.

7. Punching out the baize discs to line the sockets

4 Chinese Cube

This puzzle enjoyed a revival some years ago when tens of thousands were imported from the Far East in both cuboid and spherical forms. They re-established the popularity of the puzzle but, being mass-produced in rather mundane and unfinished woods, they lacked the visual impact that the puzzle can command. It is particularly challenging just to dismantle this puzzle and, unless one can memorise both the position of the pieces and the sequence of their removal, even more difficult to assemble. Made with care from selected woods, it can be a visually appealing project that is of interest to puzzlers and others alike. A design for a simple stand is given, on which the cube can be displayed to good effect.

Object
To dismantle and reassemble the ten pieces to form a cube.

Construction
Moderately difficult. Although the individual pieces are fairly straightforward to make, being just simple housing joints in most parts, the scale is such that small errors become significant and it is not easy to achieve the degree of precision, both of size and squareness, that the perfectly fitting puzzle demands. One plus factor is that several of the parts are pre-shaped and glued together, and that the accuracy of the recesses in some of the pieces is dimensionally less critical because their fit is concealed inside the puzzle.

Materials
Vividly contrasting woods have been used in the model photographed here, and these give the puzzle its attractive appearance. The eight corner blocks are of padauk, with other parts of sycamore and wenge. The display stand is made of teak with stainless steel rods. A closely fitting puzzle like this must, of necessity, be made of well-seasoned woods which should then be stored for some weeks in the conditions in which it will be kept.

Prepared sizes (with allowance for spare pieces)

Cubes	300 × 24mm (12 × 1in) square
Rectangular parts	580 × 18 × 12mm (23 × ¾ × ½in)
Square parts	580 × 12mm (23 × ½in) square
Base	75mm (3in) square × 13mm (½in)
Rod supports	375mm (15in) × 3mm (⅛in) dia.
Baize for base	

Method

Corner cubes
The material for these should be prepared accurately square and sufficiently long for eight cubes plus a few spare ones. The exact size is less important than the squareness, particularly if a disc sander is not available for truing up the cubes. If this machine can be used the cubes may then be marked off slightly overlong and sawn off to length. Particular accuracy is not essential as the disc sander jig (see chapter 3) will ensure that each is of uniform size and squareness (photo 1).

1. Jig sanding of the cubes ensures accuracy

Alternatively, if the cubes are to be made entirely by hand, it is worthwhile planing both ends of the wood accurately square on a shooting board with a sharp finely set plane (see chapter 3). To measure the length of each cube from the planed end use a short piece of the cube wood the *width* of which will give the correct *length*. Mark this length with a square

Marking out should be done in pencil first, then the marking gauge used from the faceside to give the depth of the slots (photo 2). The gauge is set to the *thickness* of the wood used. The pencilled lines can now be cut in, using a square and marking knife with the test piece giving the precise length of each slot. Two of the parts require further marking out in a similar way, because a second slot connects with the first. A gauge set to half the thickness of the wood – 6mm (¼in) – will give the depth of these slots. Saw down the sides of the slots, using a mitre block to ensure the squareness of the cut in both directions (photo 3). Waste from the slots can be removed with a chisel, working carefully from each side, and with the final paring cut made exactly into the gauge line. Before sawing the pieces off to length, a fine file can be used, if necessary, to smooth the base of the slots.

Square parts
Sufficient wood, and some to spare, should be prepared square in section and to the exact thickness of the rectangular parts. If the two lengths of wood (the square and the rectangular) are placed side by side on a flat surface, the fingertips will readily detect any discrepancies in thickness, and a fine shaving or two can be removed as necessary. The marking out, gauging, cutting, etc, involved in shaping these parts is as described for the rectangular ones. However, one advantage of these joints is that their fit is hidden, thus allowing a slight relaxation in the degree of precision aimed for.

Cube assemblies
Two assemblies, each of four cubes and a rectangular part, are glued together to form the major sections of the puzzle (photo 4). Some care is necessary, when gluing these together, to

and marking knife, then cut off just clear of the line with a small tenon or dovetail saw, used in conjunction with a mitre block to ensure a truly square cut. The cubes are too short to have their sawn ends planed, but they can be trued and smoothed using a sanding jig (see chapter 3).

Rectangular parts
Sufficient wood should be prepared to size, with accurately square edges, for the six parts required, plus a spare or two, and a short test piece. This will be used for its *thickness* to give the *length* of the slots when marking out.

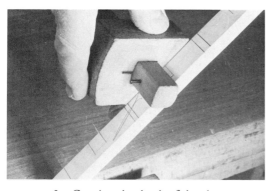

2. Gauging the depth of the slots

3. Sawing the sides of the slots with the aid of a mitre block

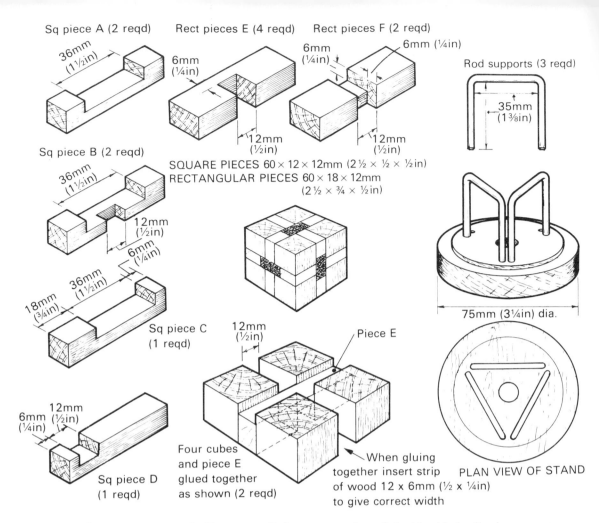

Sq piece A (2 reqd)

36mm (1½in)

Rect pieces E (4 reqd)

6mm (¼in)

12mm (½in)

Rect pieces F (2 reqd)

6mm (¼in)   6mm (¼in)

12mm (½in)

Rod supports (3 reqd)

35mm (1⅜in)

Sq piece B (2 reqd)

36mm (1½in)

12mm (½in)

6mm (¼in)

SQUARE PIECES 60 × 12 × 12mm (2½ × ½ × ½in)
RECTANGULAR PIECES 60 × 18 × 12mm
(2½ × ¾ × ½in)

36mm (1½in)

18mm (¾in)

6mm (¼in)

Sq piece C (1 reqd)

12mm (½in)

Piece E

75mm (3¼in) dia.

12mm (½in)

6mm (¼in)

Sq piece D (1 reqd)

Four cubes and piece E glued together as shown (2 reqd)

When gluing together insert strip of wood 12 x 6mm (½ x ¼in) to give correct width

PLAN VIEW OF STAND

ensure the squareness and alignment of the separate parts, otherwise 'adjustments' will have to be made at a later stage and this can only result in less well fitting parts.

One method of ensuring accuracy is to attach

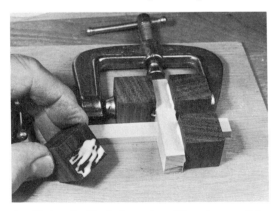

4. Gluing the blocks into place. Note the use of the thin spacing piece of wood

two strips of double-sided adhesive tape to a piece of thin card, with a gap between of about 16mm (⅝in) wide. The rectangular part should be placed squarely across the tapes with the slot bridging the gap. A thin spacing piece of wood, the same *width* as the core pieces, should now be inserted under the bridge. The four cubes can now be pressed down into position on the tape, and into close contact with the rectangular part and the spacing piece. The assembly can be lifted up and hinged open slightly, to allow a little glue to be inserted between the pieces. When it has been replaced on the flat surface, small G cramps can be used to supply a little pressure for the gluing operation. Pads of wood, usually used under G cramps to prevent marking of the surface, should not be necessary in this instance as only minimal pressure is required. Remove all excess glue with a damp cloth, before it sets. When dry, the excess length of the rectangular pieces can be pared

36

5. Sanding the pieces smooth

6. Turning the stand on a 'makeshift' lathe

away, and sanded flat on a piece of fine abrasive paper pinned to a board. The top and bottom areas of the cube assemblies can also be sanded smooth in the same way (photo 5). Some fine adjustments may have to be made with a chisel and fine file, so that all parts fit into the appropriate slots and recesses. However, this should not be indulged in too enthusiastically or general looseness may be introduced. Because the puzzle must be assembled to complete its construction, the reader should refer to chapter 7 for details.

When assembled, smoothing of the cube can be done by rubbing each side onto a sheet of abrasive, pinned to a board or, if sufficient delicacy of control can be exercised, by using a disc sander. The cube is completed by making a small chamfer on all external edges by sanding on the board or with a block plane.

Stand

This consists of a turned disc of wood with U-shaped rods inserted into it to support the cube. The sawn out disc can be mounted on a lathe face plate with double-sided tape, and the edge and the small step turned with a suitable scraper tool. Alternatively, the disc can be mounted on a mandrel and gripped in the chuck of an electric hand drill used as a makeshift lathe (photo 6).

The rod for the supports can be bent in the

vice using a hammer. Precise size is not important but they should all be identical. The triangle and the rod centres can be marked directly onto the disc, or first onto paper which can be fixed to the base of the stand and the hole centres pricked through. These are then drilled through slightly smaller than the rod size (photo 7), and opened out with a rod sized drill

7. Drilling the rod holes from the underside

to a depth of 8mm ($\frac{5}{16}$in) from the top surface. When the supports are tapped into place they will be gripped firmly by the undersized holes.

Finishing

This, and fitting the baize to the underside of the base, is dealt with in chapter 4.

5 Easy Cube

This puzzle is a far cry from its Chinese cousin, both in difficulty of construction and in finding the solution. It looks easy to solve and, in practice, the majority of puzzlers are likely to succeed in assembling it in one sitting. However, as with all tests of spatial perception, some may find that the solution will elude them for a long time, if not for ever! For lovers of wood it is a particularly attractive puzzle, with its random juxtaposition of five different polished wood species. Because the pieces do not interlock, a design for a simple stand is given on which the puzzle can be held together and displayed to good effect.

Object
To assemble the seven parts to form a cube.

Construction
Quite easy, particularly if a jig method is used to true the ends of the cubes. Minor inaccuracies will affect the appearance of the puzzle, but not its assembly. If the base is made somewhat larger, a pair of wooden dowels could be used in each corner to contain the cube, in place of the bent metal corner pillars.

Materials
Only offcut pieces are required, but for the best effect they should be chosen to contrast well with each other. The puzzle shown uses pieces of padauk, teak, yew, Macassar ebony and sycamore, mounted on a base of na. The corner pillars are made of stainless steel or brass rod.

Prepared sizes

Pieces	Total length 760 × 20/24mm (30 × ¾/1in) square Various lengths of different wood required
Base	100mm (4in) square × 16mm (⅝in)
Pillars	710mm (28in) × 3mm (⅛in) dia.
Baize for base	

Method

Cubes
The individual pieces, which are glued together to form more complex shapes, are either cuboid, double cuboid or triple cuboid in shape. It is, therefore, convenient to make the cubes first, and then the other parts exactly double or treble their length. As shown in the photograph, each assembled shape is made up from pieces of the same wood species, but different varieties could be used if preferred. Sufficient wood should be prepared, accurately square in section, for all the parts, plus some extra for spares. The precise size is unimportant, but all the pieces should be the same size in section and quite parallel along their lengths. A disc sander, with a 90° fence and a cube making jig, is the quickest and most accurate way to shape the pieces. If this facility is not available, the cube sanding jig can be used instead and will also be useful in truing the end grain of the rectangular pieces. Because hand-sanding of end grain is more laborious than planing it, both ends of each individual piece of wood should first be planed square and true on a shooting board (photo 1). Then, when the cubes and other pieces are sawn away, one

1. Planing the end of the wood square on a shooting board

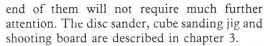

end of them will not require much further attention. The disc sander, cube sanding jig and shooting board are described in chapter 3.

The width of a short endpiece of wood should be used to mark off the *length* of each cube from a planed end. After cutting off the cubes with a tenon saw, used in conjunction with a mitre block to ensure a square cut, the sawn ends can be planed ready for marking out the next cubes or pieces. When the cubes have been made, as described in chapter 3, test assemblies of two of them, and of three, should be sellotaped together to enable these lengths to be marked off to give the length of the longer pieces. When sanding the ends of the longer pieces, they should be checked frequently against the test pieces to ensure accurate length. The cubes, and other parts, should be sanded smooth by rubbing them along a piece of fine abrasive fixed down to a board with drawing pins or double-sided adhesive tape.

Assembly

In preparation for gluing the parts together, they should be held in their correct position and sellotaped together on one side. This should be done, where possible, with the pieces resting on a flat surface to ensure perfect alignment. The drawing shows the end grain positions of the cubes, and of the pieces they are glued to. This orientation of the parts ensures that the grains will match, and that end grain surfaces are not glued to the sides of pieces. This improves both the appearance of the assembled parts and effectiveness of the gluing. The parts can now be hinged apart, and a little glue spread between them. When they have been closed together again, light G cramp pressure can be

2. Gluing the parts together

39

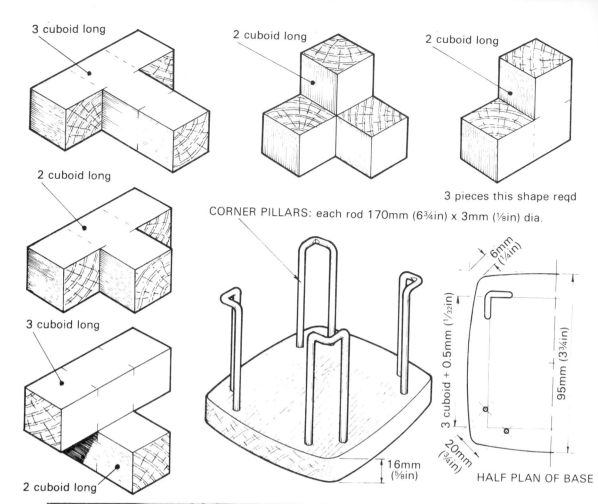

3 cuboid long

2 cuboid long

2 cuboid long

2 cuboid long

3 pieces this shape reqd

CORNER PILLARS: each rod 170mm (6¾in) x 3mm (⅛in) dia.

3 cuboid long

2 cuboid long

6mm (¼in)

3 cuboid + 0.5mm (½zin)

95mm (3¾in)

20mm (¾in)

16mm (⅝in)

HALF PLAN OF BASE

3. Sanding the parts flat

applied to hold them in position (photo 2). It is not necessary to use pads of wood under the G cramps because only minimal pressure is required, and their use can impede the gluing operation. Excess glue should be removed with a damp cloth before setting the parts aside to dry. When dry, the joints can be rubbed flat and true against a sheet of abrasive (photo 3).

Base
The shape of the base can be marked directly onto the wood or, perhaps more conveniently, on to a card template first. After cutting it out with scissors, its shape can be marked around with a pencil onto the base wood. It can be sawn out with a bandsaw or coping saw, and the edges made square and true to the line with a spokeshave or block plane. The small radiused corners can be pared with a chisel, then the outside edges sanded smooth with a fine abrasive wrapped round a block.

Corner pillars
The stainless steel rod for the pillars should be sawn off to length and the ends slightly chamfered with a file. The centre of the rod should be marked, and a small 'nick' filed on, to assist the sharp bending of the rod at this point. The rod is gripped horizontally in a metalworking vice with the nick aligned with one end of the jaws. Vice clamps of tinplate, or

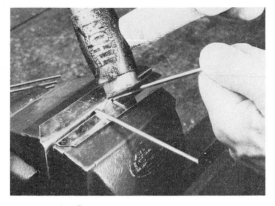

4. Bending the corner pillars

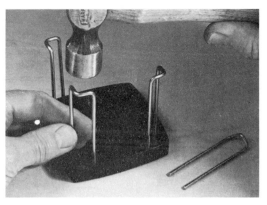

6. Tapping the corner pillar in position

5. Drilling the pillar holes in the base

other thin metal, must be used each side of the rod to protect it from the serrated jaws of the vice. The rod can now be bent sharply to a right angle with hammer blows. The bent *corner* of the rod should now be placed in the vice, with each 'leg' inclined upwards at 45°, and gripped tightly at a point when the legs are 20mm (¾in) apart and level with the top of the vice. The protruding legs are now hammered over and together, so that they become parallel with each other and square with the jaws of the vice (photo 4). The positions of the holes can be found most readily with the aid of a square piece of thin plywood cut to be slightly larger than the base size of the cube. The pillar legs can now be placed astride the corners of the square at 45°, and their positions marked on the top surface with a pencil. If the square of wood is now fixed to the top of the base with double-sided tape, the holes can be made with the drill aligned with the marks and just touching the edges of the square (photo 5). Best results are obtained if rod-sized holes are drilled 5mm (³⁄₁₆in) deep, then a slightly smaller hole drilled in deeper. The pillar rod will enter the surface hole easily and will then be gripped firmly by the smaller hole as it is tapped down in (photo 6).

Finishing
This is dealt with in chapter 4.

6 Five into One Square

At first sight this two-dimensional puzzle looks as easy to solve as its simple shaped pieces are to make. Appearances can be deceptive however, and its solution can be frustratingly protracted, except to those whose mathematical insight comes to their aid.

The pieces lend themselves well to holding and display in a rack, and a simple modern design for this is included. An alternative division of the square, the Chinese Tangram – an example of which is in the Bethnal Green Museum, London, dated 1880 – is given in the drawing, but these shapes do not lend themselves so well to storage in a rack.

Simple puzzles, such as this, can be elevated to look impressive and eyecatching if made with care, and well finished in good quality woods.

Object
To arrange the ten pieces together to form one large square.

Construction
Easy. A suitable project for the least experienced woodworker. Small inaccuracies are of little consequence and will not affect the assembly of the puzzle.

Materials
In the puzzle shown the pieces are made of end grain slices of yew. These exhibit a rich, wild grain and they contrast well with the sombre black of the Indian ebony stand. Most offcuts of timber are suitable for this project and even the usual caveat – that they must be well seasoned – is of less importance than usual.

Prepared sizes
Pieces	450 × 90 × 8mm (18 × 3½ × 5/16 in)
Stand sides	220 × 45 × 6mm (8½ × 1¾ × ¼ in)
Base	50 × 85 × 10mm (2 × 3⅜ × ⅜ in)
Rods	230mm (9in) × 3mm (⅛ in) dia.
Baize for base	

Method

Template
Two templates, each cut to the shape of the pieces, are useful when marking out, particu-larly if random shaped or waney-edged pieces of wood are being used. Metal templates, of tinplate or thin aluminium, are most convenient as just one square, with its short diagonal, can be marked and cut out (photo 1).

1. Cutting out the templates

Thin plywood, or other materials, could be used but allowance has to be made for the saw cut and for cleaning up the edges. The shapes can be marked out with pencil, orientating the template to obtain the best grained effect where appropriate (photo 2). If end grain slices of wood are used, as on the model shown, these will first require sawing off to an oversize thickness on a band or circular saw. Because it is not usually feasible to plane large areas of end

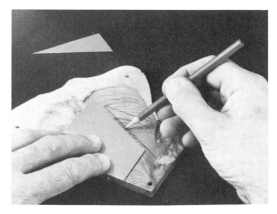

2. Marking out the pieces

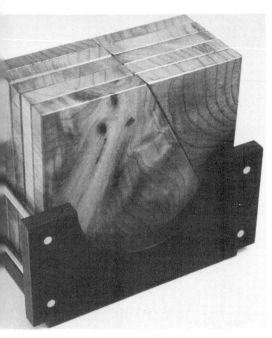

When a piece of each shape is placed together, they should, hopefully, form a square but, if not, minor inaccuracies are unimportant.

The sides of the pieces should be sanded smooth by rubbing them against a sheet of fine abrasive, fixed to a board with drawing pins or double-sided adhesive tape. The edges can be treated in a similar way, gripping each piece as low as possible to prevent rocking or tilting. Finally the edges can be slightly chamfered by tilting the pieces at 45° and dragging them lightly across the abrasive.

Rack sides

These have a semi-circular cut-out in the upper edges, and this can be cut most effectively by mounting the pieces on a faceplate and turning a hole between them. Even a makeshift lathe, using an electric hand drill on a stand with a wooden tool rest, will produce satisfactory results. The face plate can be a disc of wood, with two centre lines pencilled on at right angles to each other, and it can be mounted on a mandrel for gripping in the chuck. A 10mm (⅜in) dia. bolt, with the head sawn off, can be used as the mandrel, and the faceplate secured to it with a nut and washer on each side. The sides can be secured to the face plate with double-sided adhesive tape, which is more than adequately strong in this situation. Otherwise, the sides should be left overlong and screws used for fixing through the excess length. If necessary, semi-circular notches will require cutting into the top edges of each side, to fit around the protruding nut and washer.

The hole can be cut with a file, ground to a

grain, they can either be sanded smooth to the required thickness, using a disc sander or linisher belt, or turned on the face plate of a lathe. These procedures are not easy or straight-forward, and the use of end-grain slices is only feasible if the necessary experience and machine aids are available. The shapes can be cut out with a tenon saw on a bench hook (photo 3), or with a bandsaw, cutting clear of the lines to allow for truing up. A convenient method of truing the edges of the pieces is to plane them on the shooting board (photo 4). This ensures that they are accurately square and the lines can also be seen more easily than when planing with the workpiece in the vice.

3. Sawing the pieces to shape

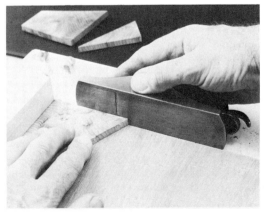

4. Planing the edges of the pieces on a shooting board

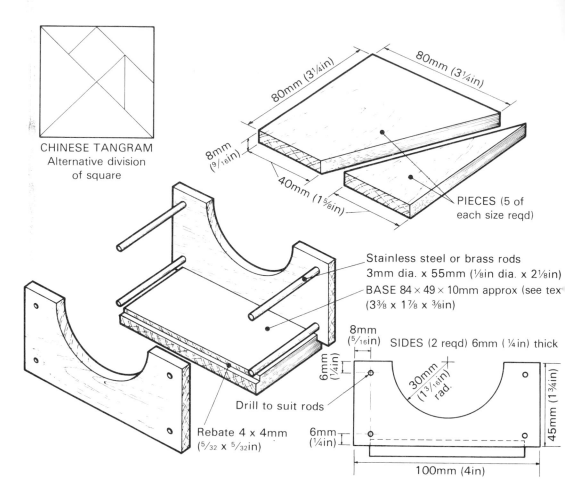

CHINESE TANGRAM
Alternative division
of square

80mm (3¼in)

80mm (3¼in)

8mm (⁹⁄₁₆in)

40mm (1⁵⁄₈in)

PIECES (5 of each size reqd)

Stainless steel or brass rods
3mm dia. x 55mm (⅛in dia. x 2⅛in)

BASE 84 × 49 × 10mm approx (see text)
(3⅜ x 1⅞ x ⅜in)

8mm (⁵⁄₁₆in) SIDES (2 reqd) 6mm (¼in) thick

6mm (¼in)

30mm (1³⁄₁₆in) rad.

45mm (1¾in)

6mm (¼in)

100mm (4in)

Drill to suit rods

Rebate 4 x 4mm
(⁵⁄₃₂ x ⁵⁄₃₂in)

skew-pointed shape with a left-hand side cutting edge incorporated, or with a skew-pointed chisel (photo 5). Precise size of the hole is unimportant, but the aim should be to obtain as good a finish as possible. This will normally be achieved just after the tool has been sharpened, as the scraping action of the tool can quite quickly dull the cutting edge. A folded piece of fine abrasive can be used to smooth the circular hole, but care should be taken not to round over the sharp edges of the hole or the crisp outline will be lost. The parts can now be levered off, or unscrewed, from the face plate and placed together as a pair. If all is well they can be secured to each other with double-sided tape and the hole positions marked on. The hole centres are given by the size of a square piece, plus one diameter of the rod to be used, plus 0.5mm (¹⁄₃₂in bare) allowance for clearance. If the rods allow a sloppy fit for the pieces they will not align themselves well in the rack, and a staggered, untidy appearance will be

the result. After the hole positions have been indented with a centre punch or nail, they are drilled to be a close fit for the rods (photo 6). A pillar drill is almost essential for this operation, to ensure true squareness of the holes with the surface. All surfaces and edges of the sides can

5. Turning the semi-circular cut-outs in the rack sides

44

now be rubbed smooth against the abrasive-covered board.

Rack base

The base width is given by the combined thickness of the five pieces plus the size of the two rebates, 8mm ($\frac{5}{16}$in), plus a small allowance for clearance, 0.5mm ($\frac{1}{32}$in bare). In length, the base aligns with the centres of the holes at each end. The wood should be prepared to these sizes with the end grain planed on the shooting board or trued on a disc sander. The extent of the rebate can be marked on with a marking or cutting gauge set to 4mm ($\frac{5}{32}$in), as shown in photo 7. The rebates can be cut with a plane, with the fence and depth gauge set to size, or with a circular saw with a rise and fall table. Planing small rebates on a short piece of wood is not an easy operation and, to overcome the difficulty, it could be laminated together from two pieces of wood. The upper piece should fit between the sides, and the lower thicker piece will overlap it to form the rebates.

Rods

These rods should be sawn off about 2mm ($\frac{5}{64}$in) overlong and the edges slightly chamfered to ensure easy entry into the holes. Stainless steel is the best metal to use, but brass is also suitable, after polishing and lacquering. Clear nail varnish can be used to lacquer the rods, and two coats will be sufficient. If the rods are a tight push fit into their holes it will not be necessary to glue them into place; if not, a

7. Marking the rebate on the base

8. G cramping the rack together

touch of rapid-setting epoxy adhesive in the holes should fix them securely. The sides should be pressed onto the rods so that the ends protrude slightly, then the base glued and G cramped into place (photo 8). A second G cramp can be used, if necessary, to press the sides into good contact in the rebate. All surplus glue should be removed with a damp cloth, and any excess epoxy resin from around the holes, with methylated spirits (wood alcohol). When dry, the protruding ends of the rods should be filed flush with a sharp, smooth-cut file. The sides can now be rubbed onto a fine abrasive sheet, to remove any file marks and give overall smoothness.

Finishing

This, and fixing baize to the underside of the rack, is dealt with in chapter 4.

6. Drilling the rod holes in the sides

7 Magic Square

Translated into wooden form from the popular paper and pencil teaser, this is a particularly eye-catching project with the advantage that it is always instantly ready for action. It is a convenient and comfortable size to hold, is fascinating to play and few can resist trying to find the solution.

The playing area features the unusual appearance and texture of wood end grain, and the inlaid appearance of the lines is readily achieved by sandwiching the blocks together with thin contrasting wood in between. Adjoining one side of the chequered area is a holder for those pegs being pondered over. The whole is contained within an edging of the same wood as the squares to give an harmonious effect to the puzzle. Turned wooden pegs, shaped for easy handling and fitted into baize-lined sockets, complete this attractive project.

Object
To arrange the pegs, numbered one to nine inclusive, so that each line, column and long diagonal adds up to fifteen.

Construction
Basically straightforward, but care and accuracy are needed to ensure that the chequered top is square, or problems will be encountered when fitting the mitred edges. The pegs can be most easily turned on a metalworking lathe but an electric hand drill, with stand, can be utilised for this if necessary.

Materials
The original used the fairly sombre combination of Indian rosewood and padauk, relieved by sycamore lines and boxwood pegs. Many other timber species could be used but it is essential that they are well seasoned or trouble will ensue. Really dense hardwoods such as ebony, boxwood, na, Lignum Vitae, etc are ideal for the pegs because they turn so well, give an excellent finish, and rub-down numbers fix to them readily.

Prepared sizes

Chequered top	200 × 24mm (8 × $^{15}/_{16}$in) square
Lines	650 × 25 × 1.5mm (26 × 1 × $^1/_{16}$in)
Peg holder	80 × 45 × 22mm (3⅛ × 1¾ × ⅞in)
Edges	475 × 25 × 8mm (19 × 1 × $^5/_{16}$in)
Pegs	600 × 20mm (24 × ¾in) square
Rub-down numbers	10mm (⅜in) or 12mm (½in) high

Baize for base and lining holes

Method

Chequered top
To make the 'squares' a piece of wood about 200mm (8in) long should be prepared accurately square in section. The precise size is not important but the squareness is! Saw this piece into three equal lengths and glue them together sideways, with pieces of thin contrasting wood in between (photo 1). The thin wood

1. The wood for the top is glued together with contrasting wood between

can be sawn off with a circular saw about 1.5mm (¹/₁₆in) thick, or be made from two or three thicknesses of veneer glued together under pressure. Initially, on tightening the G cramp, the glue will cause the pieces to slide out of alignment. If they are then pulled apart and repositioned together on a flat surface, they should remain as placed when the cramp is tightened again. Remove excess glue with a

damp cloth, and in subsequent gluing operations, before setting the work aside to dry.

Next, grip the assembly in the vice and plane both sides flat with a block plane. If the blocks were square in section originally, and glued together in alignment, little more should need planing away than shavings from the protruding 'lines'. Saw this assembly into three pieces and glue these back together with pieces of the thin wood between them, as previously, and with a piece on each side (photo 2). The vice is a convenient means of applying pressure in this

operation, and wood packing should be arranged between the jaws to bring the workpiece near the top for easier inspection and adjustment. Here care must be taken to see that the 'lines' of the separated pieces are aligned accurately. When dry, protruding 'lines' can be sawn and planed away, and the two untrued ends made ready for their 'lines' to be glued on.

The sides of the top can be made flat with a linishing machine or disc sander. They may also be planed by hand in the vice, with a sharp, finely set plane. This is not an easy operation, as the surface presented is the rather intractable end grain and also the edges are somewhat vulnerable. The best procedure is to plane diagonally inwards and lift the plane before the blade reaches the farther edge. Exact finished thickness is not critical and a flat parallel block should be the objective.

Peg holder
The piece of wood for this should be prepared very slightly oversize then glued onto one side of the chequered top. When dry it should be planed so that all surfaces are exactly level and true with each other.

2. The chequered top clamped together in the vice

47

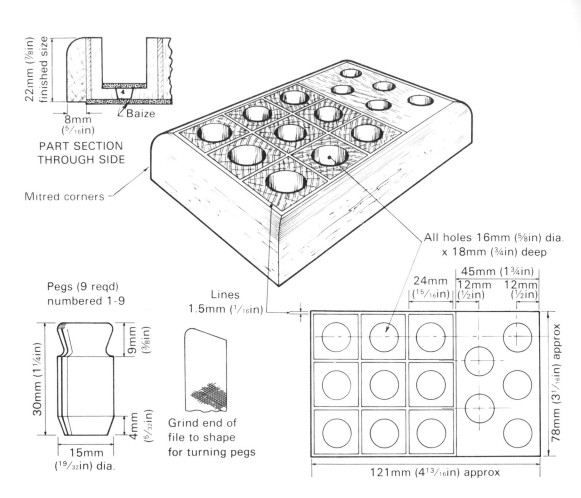

22mm (⅞in) finished size

8mm (⁵⁄₁₆in)

Baize

PART SECTION
THROUGH SIDE

Mitred corners

Pegs (9 reqd)
numbered 1-9

30mm (1¼in)

9mm (³⁄₈in)

4mm (⁵⁄₃₂in)

15mm
(¹⁹⁄₃₂in) dia.

Grind end of
file to shape
for turning pegs

Lines
1.5mm (¹⁄₁₆in)

All holes 16mm (⁵⁄₈in) dia.
x 18mm (¾in) deep

24mm
(¹⁵⁄₁₆in)

45mm (1¾in)

12mm
(½in)

12mm
(½in)

78mm (3¹⁄₁₆in) approx

121mm (4¹³⁄₁₆in) approx

Edges

These should be marked out on prepared wood, then sawn off slightly overlong to allow for trimming (photo 3). The mitres can be adjusted to fit precisely with the aid of a planing jig or with a disc sander with mitre fence attachment (see chapter 3). When three pieces have been fitted – and marked so that they can be refitted correctly – they can be sellotaped together and held in place as the last side is adjusted (photo 4). When all appears to be well, clamp together 'dry' before dismantling for gluing (photo 5).

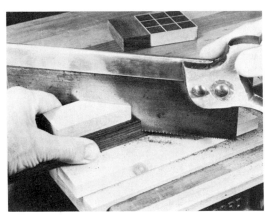

3. Sawing the mitred ends of the edging strips

4. Testing the fit of the edging strips

48

5. Clamping the edging in place 'dry' prior to gluing

6. Drilling the peg holes

Vice pressure is used for the sides and a sash clamp for the ends. The overwide edging strips make alignment with the top less critical than usual, but they should overlap on the underside to provide a small recess for the baize. When dry, the edges should be planed flush with the top and to give the aforementioned overlap on the underside. The top edges can be rounded with a block plane, either at this stage or when the peg holes have been drilled.

Peg holes
The hole positions are marked with a pencil and drilled with a 16mm (⅝in) flat bit. If possible, this should be done with a bench or pillar drill to ensure that they are drilled square with the surface and to the correct depth (photo 6). The point of the bit will penetrate the underside, but as this, and the holes, will be lined with baize this is of no consequence.

Pegs
These should be made of the hardest available wood and of a species to give good contrast with the base. If a lathe is not available, they can be turned with the aid of an electric hand drill (with stand), using a wooden tool rest. One method of mounting short pieces of wood in a drill chuck is first to drill a hole in the end grain, then glue in a short spigot of dowel to protrude about 30mm (1¼in). Dowel 10mm (⅜in) dia. will suit most chucks and the holes should be about 16mm (⅝in) deep. Alternatively, overlong pieces of pegwood can have one end reduced to a diameter suitable for gripping in the chuck by using a chisel or rasp. Turning down to diameter can be done with a chisel or scraping tool and should be checked with callipers. The shaped end can be formed most

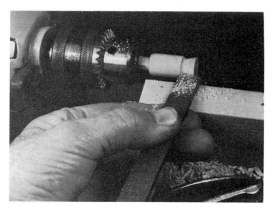

7. Turning the pegs with scraping tool

easily and consistently by using a scraping tool ground to shape from an old file (photo 7). The profile for this tool is given in the drawing, and the left hand slope of the tool is the correct angle for shaping the tapered end of the peg. Well smooth each peg in the lathe then part them off to length. The rub-down numbers will be easier to apply if a hole is drilled in a block of wood, deep enough to bring the pegs flush with the surface. The numbers can be sealed permanently in place with two or three coats of white French polish (shellac) applied with a soft brush.

Finishing
Polishing and fixing baize on the underside is dealt with in chapter 4. A nice touch is to line the holes with small discs of baize. These can be cut out with a sharpened piece of tube hammered down into the *end* grain of a block of wood. If double-sided adhesive tape is first fixed to the strip of baize, each disc will have a clean adhesive surface attached ready for pressing into the holes.

8 Puzzle Cubes

This intriguing puzzle is as visually attractive as it is frustratingly difficult to solve. It can be made with six cubes, but this four-cube version is sufficiently testing to defeat the patience and application of most people. The sides of the cubes have to be readily distinguishable and this is usually done by numbers, letters or colours. In this design, however, two original and distinctive treatments are suggested, both of which will produce heirloom quality puzzles that are a delight to handle and display. One is to veneer the sides with contrasting woods, and the other is to inlay the sides of the cubes with a series of polished coins. A stand to hold and display the set of four cubes is required, and alternative designs are given for this.

Object
To arrange the cubes in their holder with four different coins or four different woods showing on each side.

Construction
Quite easy, particularly if a mechanical aid can be used for shaping the cubes. Some adjustments have to be made to the flat bits to cut coin-sized recesses, but this is simple to accomplish by trial and error using a grindstone or a file.

Materials
The coin puzzle shown has cubes of Spanish olive held in a stand of Indian ebony. The wild attractive grain of the olive contrasts well with the sombre black of the stand. The alternative cubes are veneered in Macassar ebony, padauk, satinwood and sycamore which were chosen to be as distinctive as possible from each other. The stand design shown with the veneered cubes is made of Honduras mahogany, although either stand can, of course, be used with either set of cubes. The material requirements for either version of the puzzle are unusually modest and only offcut-sized pieces of wood are needed.

Prepared sizes

Cubes (4)	250 × 38mm (10 × 1½in) square
Veneer offcuts	44mm (1¾in) square
Perforated base stand	Base 180 × 40 × 6mm (7 × 1⁹⁄₁₆ × ¼in)
	Ends 60 × 50 × 6mm (2⅜ × 2 × ¼in)
Vee stand	Base 180 × 35 × 6mm (7 × 1⅜ × ¼in)
	Ends 100 × 55 × 6mm (4 × 2⅛ × ¼in)
Rods (4 or 2)	Each 170mm (6¾in) × 3mm (⅛in) dia.
Coins	24 required
Baize for base	

Method

Cubes
It is necessary to make the cubes first because the stand can then be custom-made to fit a set of four. Any plain, but well-seasoned, hardwood can be used for veneered cubes, but that selected for coin cubes should be chosen for its colour, striking grain and contrast with the coins. Softwood, with the possible exception of yew, is not recommended for the cubes because they can suffer considerable damage to the corners and edges, if dropped. If the cubes can be trued with the aid of a disc sander and jig, great accuracy in preparing the square sectional wood is unnecessary. Otherwise, if the cubes

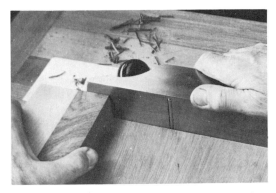

1.   Planing the square ends on the cube wood

50

are to be handmade, it is advisable to plane the wood to be parallel and as square as possible. Although the cube sanding jig will greatly assist in making accurate cubes it is, nevertheless, worthwhile planing the ends of the cube material on a shooting board (photo 1). The *length* of each cube can be marked, using the *width* of a short endpiece of the wood, to give the size. The pieces can be sawn off squarely, and just clear of the line, with a tenon saw (photo 2), using a mitre block. Each cube can now be trued on the cube sanding jig (photo 3), using the coarse side of the abrasive block initially to deal with the sawn end, then smoothing all the sides with the fine abrasive.

Alternatively, all the cubes can be sawn off slightly overlong, then sanded precisely square and to uniform size with the disc sander jig (photo 4). Details of the disc sander, cube sanding jig, shooting board and mitre block are given in chapter 3.

Veneered cubes
Reference to the chart will give the number of pieces of veneer of each species required, and these can be cut to size with scissors. The illustration of the cube 'flattened' out will give the positions of the veneers, and the initials of each veneer should be marked on each side with a pencil. Squares of thick plywood or chipboard

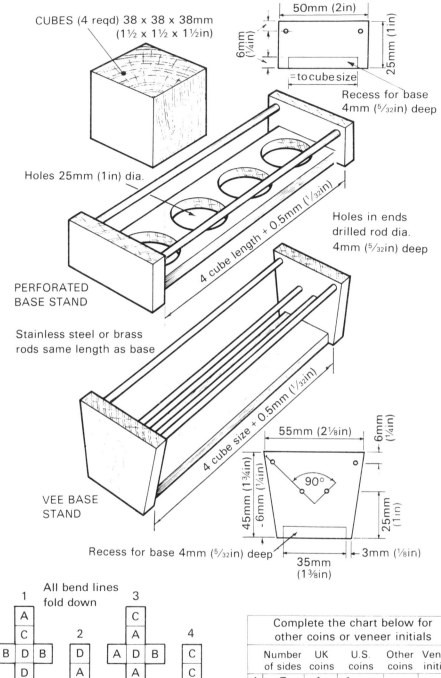

CUBES (4 reqd) 38 x 38 x 38mm
(1½ x 1½ x 1½in)

50mm (2in)

6mm (¼in)

25mm (1in)

= to cube size

Recess for base
4mm (⁵/₃₂in) deep

Holes 25mm (1in) dia.

4 cube length + 0.5mm (¹/₃₂in)

Holes in ends
drilled rod dia.
4mm (⁵/₃₂in) deep

PERFORATED
BASE STAND

Stainless steel or brass
rods same length as base

4 cube size + 0.5mm (¹/₃₂in)

VEE BASE
STAND

55mm (2⅛in)

6mm (¼in)

90°

45mm (1¾in) - 6mm (¼in)

25mm (1in)

Recess for base 4mm (⁵/₃₂in) deep

3mm (⅛in)

35mm (1⅜in)

All bend lines fold down

1
A
C
B D B
D

2
D
A
B A C
C

3
C
A
A D B
A
B B A
D

4
C
C
B B A
D

Number each cube 1, 2, 3 and 4. Sketch
similar diagram to that above and
substitute coin value, or veneer initials
for the letters given. Transfer information onto cubes

Complete the chart below for other coins or veneer initials				
Number of sides	UK coins	U.S. coins	Other coins	Veneer initials
A	7	1p	1 cent		
B	6	2p	5 cent		
C	6	5p	10 cent		
D	5	10p	25 cent		

52

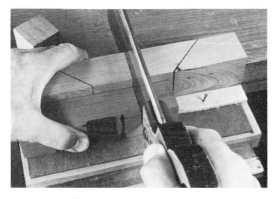

2. Sawing the cubes to length

5. Veneering the sides of the cubes

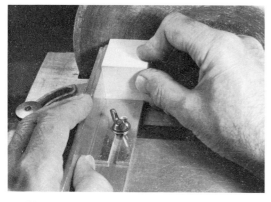

3. Truing the cubes on the cube sanding jig

6. Trimming away the overlapping veneer

4. Using the disc sander to produce accurate cubes

are used over the veneers as the opposite sides are glued down under G cramp pressure (photo 5). It is wise to place squares of paper over the veneers to obviate glue penetration problems. These can occur with certain species of veneer – burrs, bird's eye maple and others with very short-grain characteristics – if the glue is thin, or when excessive pressure is applied to the cramps. When dry, the overlapping veneer can be trimmed away with scissors, but care must

be exercised or the veneer can be split away. One blade should be held in close contact with the outer surface of the veneer, as the other blade moves to shear the veneer safely away (photo 6). The sides adjacent to those veneered should be smoothed by rubbing them down onto a fine abrasive paper held flat on a board. The next pair of sides can then be veneered. When all have been completed, the sides can be made smooth by rubbing the now veneered surfaces against the sheet of abrasive. The usual method of sanding, with the abrasive sheet wrapped over a cork block, is not suitable in this instance because it is unlikely to produce an accurately flat surface. Next, the edges should be very slightly chamfered by holding each cube at 45° to the board and lightly dragging each edge over the abrasive.

Coin cubes
By reference to the chart and to the illustrations of the 'flattened' out cubes, the value of the coins can be marked onto the sides of each cube with a soft pencil. If coins of a different currency are to be used a similar chart can be

53

drawn, and these coin values marked on the sides of the cubes.

The most convenient tool for cutting the coin recesses is a flat bit. The standard sizes of these bits will not, of course, cut recesses exactly the right size to fit the coins, but the nearest size can be modified to suit. If the coin is a little too small, a step, a little over the thickness of the coin, can be filed or ground away on the corners of the bit. Reduce the stepped width, and hence the diameter of the hole, until a trial drilling indicates that a good press fit for the coin has been obtained. Conversely, if the coin is a little too large for the bit, one *side* of the point can be filed away. This effectively increases the *radius* of the cut on one side of the bit and gives a larger hole. Flat bits are tolerant of such 'abuses' and they can be readily restored to their original size by grinding or filing. If possible, the recesses should be cut using the flat bit in a pillar drill (photo 7). If the coins are a good fit

7. Drilling the coin cube

in their recesses, and firmly gripped by their edges, the holes can be drilled more than adequately deep for the coins. If a coin is a less good fit, or even loose, the hole should be drilled to just the thickness of the coin, which can then be fixed in later with an epoxy resin adhesive. After cutting all the recesses, the sides can be smoothed by rubbing each on a fine abrasive sheet fixed down to a board.

Coins
It is preferable to use uncirculated coins and these can often be obtained from banks or Post Offices, if sufficient notice of the request is given. Used coins can be polished with metal polish and a cloth, after fixing them down to a board with double-sided adhesive tape. All coins should be cleaned with methylated spirit (wood alcohol), or detergent and warm water,

and then protected with clear cellulose lacquer. Clear nail varnish is also quite suitable for this and is, of course, very readily available.

Each coin should be tapped gently to just engage it in its recess. They can be pressed fully home using vice pressure, with a piece of thin leather or baize covering each side to protect the coins and the surrounding surface (photo 8).

8. Squeezing the coins fully home into their recesses

Stands
Two alternative designs are given and each can be used with both types of cube. The perforated base version requires the stand to be inverted to view the cubes, whereas the vee type stand allows all four sides to be seen more readily. The base wood should be prepared to the width as given in the drawing or, in the case of the perforated base model, with its width equal to the cube size. The length should be equal to the combined length of four cubes plus 9mm (³⁄₈in bare). This measurement allows for the joint at each end and for a small clearance between each cube. The positions of the view holes in the perforated version should be marked, and the holes drilled, with a flat or forstner bit (photo 9). If a flat bit is used, a piece of waste wood should be attached to the underside of the base with double-sided adhesive tape. This will prevent the problems that can arise when a relatively large flat bit breaks through the underside of the wood being drilled.

Ends
It may be found more convenient to prepare the wood for the smaller rectangular ends in one piece, and to cut the recesses for the base in each end. These can be chiselled out with the wood G cramped down to the bench. The holes

54

9. Drilling the viewing holes in the perforated base stand

10. Drilling the rod holes in the vee base stand

in the ends should be drilled 4mm (⁵⁄₃₂in) deep (photo 10). The holes in the rectangular ends should allow the cubes to be an easy fit between them.

Rods

These can be sawn off to the same length as the base, and their ends slightly chamfered by filing. If brass rods are used they must be polished with metal polish, then lacquered to prevent tarnishing.

Assembly

It is convenient to use vice pressure when assembling the stand, both to squeeze the ends squarely onto the rods and to hold the base in place during gluing (photo 11). Surplus glue should be removed with a damp cloth before it sets.

11. Gluing the stand together in the vice

Finishing

This is dealt with generally in chapter 4. Because baize cannot be so readily fixed to the underside of the perforated base stand, a small rectangle of baize can be glued near each end instead.

9 Number Sequence

This entertaining little puzzle has become familiar again in recent years, with hundreds of thousands imported from the Far East. The construction of these is such that their life, albeit a happy one, is limited, and they are soon broken and cast aside. Hopefully, this proliferation has not devalued the intrinsic appeal of the puzzle which certainly merits a more permanent form. Made in attractive and well-finished hardwoods, this is an aesthetically pleasing and easily-handled version which will amuse generations of puzzlers.

Object

To arrange the numbers in sequence in columns or rows. Many variations are possible, including arrangement in reverse order and alternating odd and even numbers.

Construction

Not easy, but quite straightforward if jig methods are used to produce accurately square blocks. This proviso also applies to making the mitred corners of the tray.

Materials

The original is made with blocks of Macassar ebony contained within a tray of olive. This ebony is not jet black, but has an attractive grain and contrasts well with the white numbers and with the richly wild grain of the olive. Most hardwoods are suitable for this puzzle, but that for the blocks should contrast well with the rub-down numbers. Although these numbers are obtainable in several colours, black, white and gold are probably the most suitable ones to choose for this project.

Prepared sizes

Number blocks	450 × 20 × 10mm (18 × ¾ × ⅜in)
Tray sides	430 × 18 × 10mm (17 × ¹¹/₁₆ × ⅜in)
Base	90mm (3½in) square × 10mm (⅜in)
Numbers	12mm (½in) size
Baize for base	

Method

Number blocks

It is necessary to make these first, then to construct the tray to fit. Sufficient wood, of a contrasting colour to the rub-down numbers, should be prepared for sixteen blocks plus several spares. It must be accurately parallel and of even thickness, but the precise size is not too important. If a disc sander is available this can be used, in conjunction with a jig, to give accurately square blocks with the minimum of effort. In this case the blocks can be sawn off just a little longer than they are wide, then trued with the aid of the jig. By hand, similar accuracy can be obtained with the aid of a cube sanding jig. It is worthwhile sawing off the blocks quite accurately to length, as subsequent sanding to size is done by hand and can be laborious if the blocks are cut generously overlong. One method, which saves the trouble of marking off each block to length, is to nail a stop onto a mitre block to allow each piece to be cut off just a fraction overlong. The position of the stop can be set with the aid of a short piece of the block wood, using its *width* to determine the length.

The blocks can now be sawn off with a fine toothed tenon saw (photo 1). The sanding of the sawn ends can be done on the cube sanding jig,

1. Sawing off the number blocks

using the coarse abrasive side initially, then finishing with the fine side (photo 2). Because the sanding marks, left by the sanding jig, are not with the grain but diagonally across it, it is necessary to smooth all sides and surfaces of the blocks by rubbing them against a sheet of fine abrasive paper, pinned down to a board. Next, the corners and edges should be very slightly radiused by rotating each edge against the abrasive as the block is drawn over it. Final smoothing can be effected by rubbing the cubes with fine steel wool.

The finished blocks should be assembled into a square and held together by an elastic band to enable their combined size to be measured (photo 3). A more pleasing overall effect is given if the grain of each block is arranged to be at right angles to its neighbours. This will also help minimise any problems that may arise if the wood used is not fully seasoned and slight shrinkage of the blocks occurs. Details of jigs and devices helpful in cube making and mitre jointing are given in chapter 3.

2. Using the cube sanding jig to produce accurately square number blocks

3. Measuring the overall size of the number blocks

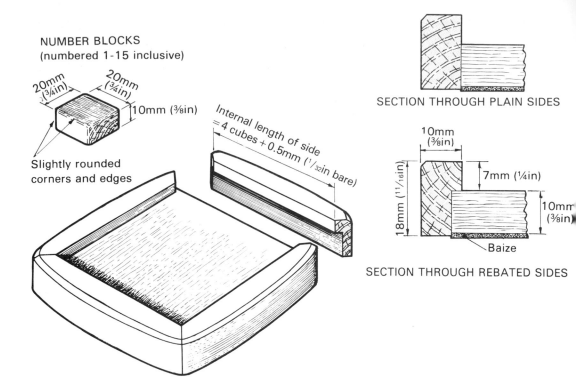

NUMBER BLOCKS
(numbered 1-15 inclusive)

20mm (¾in)
20mm (¾in)
10mm (⅜in)

Slightly rounded
corners and edges

Internal length of side
= 4 cubes + 0.5mm (1/32in bare)

SECTION THROUGH PLAIN SIDES

10mm (⅜in)
18mm (11/16in)
7mm (¼in)
10mm (⅜in)
Baize

SECTION THROUGH REBATED SIDES

Tray sides

The wood for these can be rebated to receive the base, or not, as preferred. A rebate is not necessary for reasons of strength because the thick base wood affords generous gluing contact with the sides. The size of the square plus 0.5mm (1/32in bare) should be marked on the inside surfaces of the tray sides, and sawn off on a mitre block with a tenon saw (photo 4). The mitres can be trued with a disc sander with fence attachment, or by planing on the mitre shooting board. If a mitre is planed to be slightly too short, this can be remedied by taking a shaving or two off the inner surface which will, in effect, lengthen the side. When all the mitres have been planed, they can be sellotaped together and fitted over the block. The small clearance previously mentioned should give well fitting blocks when they have been polished. If all is well, the edges can be laid out flat, glue applied to the mitres (photo 5), then the frame bound around with further layers of sellotape. Surplus glue should be removed with a damp cloth and the squareness of the frame checked, before it is set aside to dry.

4. Sawing the mitred ends of the tray sides

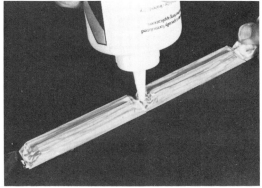

5. Gluing the mitred joints

6. G cramping the base in place

7. Chamfering the top edges of the tray

Base

This should be cut to size and, if fitted into rebated sides, can be glued and G cramped in place when a satisfactory fit has been obtained (photo 6). Its thickness should be such that the sides overlap it slightly, to give a small recess for the baize. When gluing the base to non-rebated sides, it should be pressed upwards slightly to give the required recess. Some of the waste from the curved edges and corners of the tray can be removed with a bandsaw, or by paring with a chisel. These edges can then be made smooth and true with a spokeshave or block plane. The small chamfer around the top edge can be formed with a spokeshave (photo 7), then all edges smoothed with a fine abrasive wrapped over a block.

Finishing

This is dealt with generally in chapter 4. A suitable finish for the number blocks is white or transparent French (shellac) polish. Two coats should be applied to the block with a soft brush, then each rubbed down with fine steel wool. The rub-down numbers can now be applied, and it is convenient to do this with the blocks in place in the tray, as they present a flat surrounding surface which helps to keep the number backing sheet flat. Two or three further coats of polish will protect the numbers from wear, and the last coat should be lightly smoothed with steel wool, then a little wax polish applied. If it is felt that the number blocks move too freely within the tray, a square of baize can be glued in to dampen down the movement.

10 Six Piece Chinese Puzzle

This is a classic Chinese puzzle and deservedly so. Variations of the puzzle exist with as many as nineteen pieces – and even more – but as just six pieces defeat all but a few would-be assemblers it seems somewhat pointless to make it still more difficult. Part of its charm is that most people are unwilling to admit defeat because its difficulty is so deceptive. In effect there are only five pieces to be assembled, the sixth being merely the key or locking piece which is inserted at the end. Carefully made and finished in fine quality timber, it can be a strikingly attractive puzzle that will excite interest and comment.

Object
To assemble the pieces as shown in the photograph. Without the illustration it could be described as a pair of pieces placed vertically, a pair placed north–south and a pair east–west – interlocking where they meet.

Construction
Fairly easy – in essence just a series of cross halving joints – but accuracy is necessary to achieve really pleasing results. Readers with a rise and fall circular saw, a radial arm saw or a router will find the construction much simplified by their use.

Materials
The version shown above is made of Macassar ebony. This is an attractive black, grey and beige stripy timber, quite unlike the plain black variety familiar to most people as ebony. It is much less hard than the true ebonies and can be handsawn and chiselled quite readily. With this type of puzzle, where parts are repeatedly assembled (usually incompletely!) and dismantled, it is better to use a firm hardwood to minimise wear and consequent slackness in the fit of the parts. It is also important to use well-seasoned timber acclimatised to the moisture content of the home. If this is not done a newly made and well fitted puzzle can quickly

deteriorate into a sloppily fitted one if in a centrally heated home.

Prepared sizes
750 × 24mm (30 × 1in) square

Method

The wood should be prepared accurately square in section, and long enough to make at least seven pieces, plus a short end for use as a test piece. The precise size of the square is not important and can be larger or smaller as preferred. An extra piece or two allows an immediate replacement to be made without the delay involved in preparing more wood to the precise size of that spoilt.

The *width* of the test piece is used to give the *length* of several of the slots and a similar but narrower piece is required to give the length of the shorter slots. This second piece (photo 1)

1. Accurately prepared half-width test piece gives length of shorter slots

should be prepared to exactly half the width of the full-sized test piece. Using test pieces for marking out the slots, instead of a rule, gives greater accuracy and convenience. For instance if the wood has been prepared to 23.75mm square – or some equally awkward imperial size – it is difficult to measure this slot size, and also its half-size, with a rule.

3. A marking knife is used to cut in the precise width of the slots

Unlike those in most woodwork projects, puzzle 'joints' are not glued and therefore require a more precise degree of fit than otherwise. For this reason a familiar 'dodge' to ensure that the saw cuts are made accurately to the line should be employed here. It involves chiselling a small sloping groove in the waste wood to meet the marking knife cut (photo 4).

4. Chiselling the sloping groove used to ensure precise position of saw cuts

The pieces should be marked out in pencil, initially, using the test pieces to give the lengths of the slots and with the square held firmly against the face side or face edge as appropriate. The depth of the slots can now be marked on with a marking or cutting gauge set to half the thickness of the wood (photo 2). Check the setting of the marking gauge with the narrow test piece; it should, of course, be identical. The waste to be removed should be clearly indicated with hatched pencil lines. A white pencil has been used in the photographs and these marks show up clearly on the dark wood. All the lines can now be cut in with a marking knife using the test pieces to give the exact positions of the slots (photo 3).

Also useful, unless one is an experienced woodworker, is a mitre block to ensure the squareness of the cuts as the slots are sawn (photo 5).

A small bandsaw is useful for removing waste wood from the slots, particularly the wider ones (photo 6). Alternatively a coping saw could be used or the waste easily chiselled away. Finishing chisel cuts from each side can be made with the wood held in the vice (photo 7). This allows more control and the chisel can be given a slicing action more easily than when paring out the slots vertically. Final cuts should be made with the chisel edge placed accurately

2. Gauging the depth of the slots

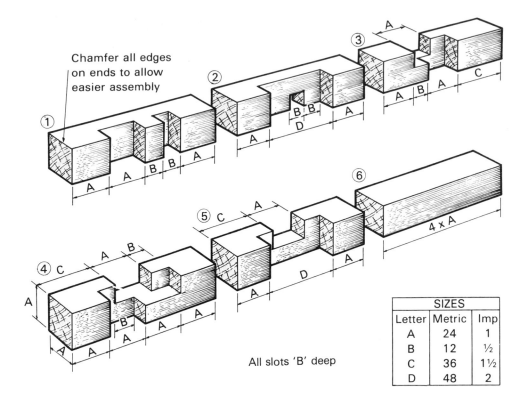

Chamfer all edges on ends to allow easier assembly

All slots 'B' deep

SIZES		
Letter	Metric	Imp
A	24	1
B	12	½
C	36	1½
D	48	2

5. Mitre block ensures squareness when sawing slot sides

6. Some slot waste can be removed by sawing

in the gauge line. The width of the chisel used in this operation is not dependent solely on the width of the slot. As shown, a narrow chisel may be preferred if a particularly hard wood is used or if the grain is interlocking. If chiselling across the grain has left roughness in the slot, this can be removed with a small smooth cut file (photo 8). Unlike the other four pieces, number 4 requires a recess cut in it which must be chiselled out. Some waste could be drilled away

first if desired, but chiselling alone will cope with it quite quickly.

The pieces can now be sawn apart and the end grain made square and true. This can be done most easily with a disc sander with the fence set accurately to 90° (photo 9), planed on a shooting board, or with the aid of the cube sanding jig (see chapter 3). If the various procedures have been done accurately all the parts should be a good push fit together in all

7. Chiselling out the slots

9. Ends of pieces are sanded square and smooth

8. Filing smooth if necessary

10. Sanding the sides of blocks smooth

appropriate slots. If this is not so, check carefully before using a chisel or file to ease the fit. It is important only to reduce the oversize part or enlarge the undersized slot and the location of the fault should be determined by the test pieces.

It is normally better not to attempt to widen slots by filing unless one is quite expert in the use of this tool. A slightly rounded surface can easily be made; generally a sharp chisel will produce a better result.

When a snug interchangeable fit has been achieved with all the parts, they can be lightly sanded to remove marks and pencil lines and to give an easier sliding fit which will allow for the thickness – albeit minimal – of the finish applied. This sanding should be done with each part rubbed along a piece of fine abrasive paper pinned to a board (photo 10). The parts can now have their end edges slightly chamfered to permit easier alignment when assembling the puzzle, and to minimise damage if the parts are dropped.

Finishing
This is dealt with in chapter 4.

11 Steady Hand Puzzle

The popularity of 'steady hand' puzzles is evident from the number and variety of these novelties available today. This design in polished hardwoods, unlike many of the plastic versions, looks smart enough to deserve a favoured place in the home. In the last century similar puzzles were called 'pigs in clover', and were commonly made in metal although at least one wooden model survives. It is a puzzle that will appeal to all members of the family, and is pleasing to look at and pleasant to handle.

Object
To manoeuvre the seven steel balls to rest in the small indentations in the base by tilting the puzzle.

Construction
Quite simple. A high standard of accuracy is not necessary to produce an effective puzzle. For readers without access to a lathe, an alternative mode of construction is suggested which will provide a recess in the top layer to receive the transparent panel.

Materials
The original puzzle shown in the photograph is made of padauk sandwiched on each side with sycamore. This combination is strikingly colourful but does give some problems with finishing, because the padauk can bleed a strong dye and discolour the sycamore. Many other contrasting wood species are suitable or, for a quieter effect, the same variety used for all three layers.

Prepared sizes

Top	170 × 125 × 6mm (6¾ × 5 × ¼in)
Base	125 × 125 × 6mm (5 × 5 × ¼in)
Centre section	150 × 120 × 12mm (6 × 4¾ × ½in)
Steel balls	six ⅜in dia. and one ⁷/₁₆in dia., or seven ⅜in dia.
Transparent panel	110mm (4⅜in) dia. × 3mm (⅛in) thick
Baize for underside of base	

Method

Centre section
The wood for the centre section should be prepared to width and thickness but a little overlong. It is suggested that the centres of the holes should be marked onto a card template first, but they can be marked directly on the wood if preferred. Use compasses to inscribe the inner circle first, then the outer concentric one. Without altering the compass setting 'step off' the radius into the circumference to give six

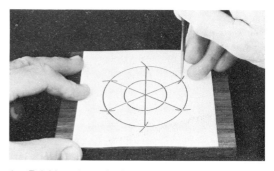

1. Pricking through the template to locate the hole positions

2. Drilling the passageway holes

equal divisions. Opposite points on the circle are now connected by lines to give six divisions on the inner circle also. If a template has been made, mark through it with a sharp point to give the thirteen hole centres (photo 1).

3. Drilling the large centre and radial holes

4. Chiselling out the passageways

Drill the smaller holes first with a twist drill or flat bit, used in a pillar drill if possible (photo 2). These holes remove most of the waste from the passageways between the centre and radial holes. When drilling the large holes (photo 3) it is necessary to secure waste wood directly to the underside of the piece being drilled or quite alarming problems can arise when large flat bits break through the wood. The waste wood can be secured with double-sided adhesive tape, or it may be pinned to the excess length of the centre section.

The passageways can be pared out easily and accurately using a chisel against a strip of wood as a guide (photo 4). The strip should be held down firmly in alignment with the edges of the small holes. A small sharp file is useful when finishing the sides of the slots, and the large holes can be sanded smooth with abrasive paper wrapped over a piece of round wood. The excess length of the centre section can be sawn away and the end grain planed square and true.

Base
Use the template to locate the positions of the centre and radial holes onto the slightly oversize base wood. These positions are countersunk (photo 5) to give the 'at rest' positions for the balls. The size across the countersink should be about 2mm ($5/64$in) and very slightly more for the centre hole, if an optional larger ball is to be used in this position.

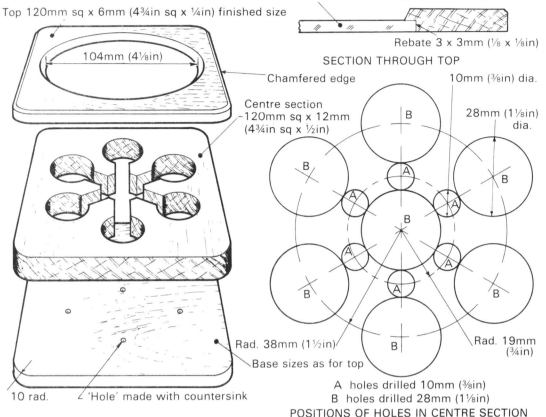

Top 120mm sq x 6mm (4¾in sq x ¼in) finished size

104mm (4⅛in)

Transparent panel approx 110mm (4⅜in) dia.

Rebate 3 x 3mm (⅛ x ⅛in)

SECTION THROUGH TOP

Chamfered edge

10mm (⅜in) dia.

Centre section 120mm sq x 12mm (4¾in sq x ½in)

28mm (1⅛in) dia.

Rad. 38mm (1½in)

Base sizes as for top

Rad. 19mm (¾in)

10 rad.   'Hole' made with countersink

A holes drilled 10mm (⅜in)
B holes drilled 28mm (1⅛in)

POSITIONS OF HOLES IN CENTRE SECTION

Top

The wood for the top has a circular hole and recess, or rebate, turned in it to receive the acrylic (Perspex, Orroglas, etc) disc. It should be well overlong initially, or problems can arise with the fragile short grain between the hole and the ends of the wood.

The top piece can be located centrally onto a wooden disc attached to the lathe face plate, if a small hole is drilled in each and a panel pin is used to align them. The top can be secured with double-sided tape or by small screws through the overlong ends near each corner. The hole and recess can both be turned with a skew pointed chisel (photo 6). With the tool rest removed, a small folded piece of fine abrasive paper should be used to smooth the edge of the hole.

If a lathe is not avaiable to cut the hole, drill a small hole through to locate the centre on both sides. The dividers are set to mark the hole size on the top and the rebate size underneath. If the

5. Countersinking the 'holes' in the base

marking leg of the dividers is sharp, and considerable pressure used, it should be possible to cut quite deeply into the wood which greatly facilitates cutting out the rebate by hand. The hole can now be made with a coping saw and its edge smoothed and bevelled with a round based

6. Turning the hole and recess in the top

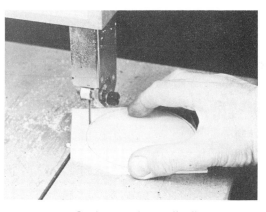

7. Sawing out the acrylic disc

spokeshave. A cutting or marking gauge, set to the thickness of the transparent disc, can now be used inside the hole. With the top clamped down to the bench it is now possible to chisel out the rebate quite easily. This operation can be made even easier by using a thinner transparent disc than the 3mm (⅛in) suggested.

Most acrylic sheet is protected by a paper covering and the size of the disc can be marked onto this with compass. Hold a small pad of wood in place to prevent the point of the compass leaving a mark. The disc can be cut out with a bandsaw (photo 7) or coping saw.

Assembly
Some wood finishing is necessary before the sandwich of parts can be glued together. These are those that show on the centre section through the top, much of the base and the edges of the hole in the top. A reliable and rapidly drying finish is white French polish (shellac)

9. Clamping arrangement for top

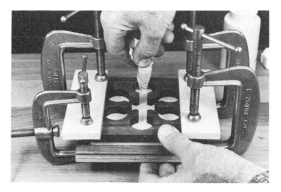

8. Gluing base to centre section

which is easily applied with a soft brush. All coats, including the last, should be smoothed with well used, very fine abrasive or 00 grade

steel wool, then rubbed with a wax polish.

When gluing the centre section to the base piece, arrange the clamps so that all the holes are easily visible. This allows any excess glue that exudes into them to be removed with a damp cloth before it sets (photo 8). When dry, drop in the seven steel balls and glue the top on. The set up for this is shown with the disc and top in front (photo 9). An extra clamp on each side would be useful for ensuring good contact. When dry, trim off the overlapping top and base flush with the centre section, and radius the corners. A block plane is useful for planing the small chamfer around the top edge of the puzzle. Use a small sanding block and fine abrasive to smooth down the puzzle ready for polishing. Care should be exercised, when sanding, to avoid rounding over the crisp edges of the chamfered top.

Finishing
This is dealt with in chapter 4.

12 Three Piece Chinese Puzzle

This has been called a Chinese puzzle, but whether or not its origin can be credited to China is uncertain. What is clear, however, is that it is a relatively simple puzzle both to make and solve. Although the construction is somewhat different, it is a good piece to make before moving on to its six piece stable companion. It is also encouraging to have some success in assembling a puzzle – a possibility that this one offers – before moving on to solve the infinitely more difficult six piece Chinese puzzle.

Object
To assemble the pieces, as shown in the photograph, consisting of one vertical piece, one arranged north–south and one east–west.

Construction
Easy and straightforward to make with hand tools, but care is necessary to achieve accurately fitting parts.

Materials
The puzzle shown here is made of Brazilian tulip wood. This is a singularly beautiful timber with pale pink stripes on a light background. Its hardness is an advantage in a puzzle which will be assembled and dismantled frequently, but is not so useful when chiselling out the mortice-like slots. Almost all hardwoods are suitable. The less experienced woodworker should select a firm but easily worked variety in order to achieve the best results.

Prepared sizes
360 × 39 × 13mm (14 × 1½ × ½in)

Method

The wood for this puzzle must be accurately prepared, to be quite parallel in both width and depth, and to have square edges. Precise sizes are less important. This is easy to achieve if a circular saw is available to cut the wood but, with care, it can be done by hand. If difficulty is experienced in planing the edges square, the wood can be held down on a shooting board and planed in this way.

Before marking out, saw off a short test piece from one end of the wood and use the *width* of this to give the *length* of each mortice. All marking out should be done, initially, in pencil with the square held firmly against the face edge (photo 1). The widths of the mortices can

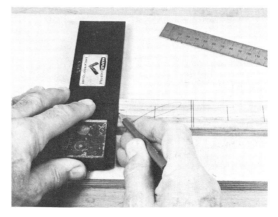

1. Initial marking out in pencil

now be marked on each side with the mortice gauge spurs set accurately to the thickness of the wood. Check, before marking, that the spurs are sharp and, if they require attention, this can be done with a smooth file. Also check, from each edge of the wood, that the mortice will be exactly in the centre of the wood. It may be found easier to hold the stock of the gauge tightly against the face edge, if the piece of wood is held in the vice (photo 2). Take care that the gauged lines do not extend beyond the pencilled lines indicating the mortice length.

With the widths of the mortices marked, the lengths can now be cut in with a marking knife. Do this first to one end of each mortice, then use the test piece to give the *precise* length of the mortice which is then marked (photo 3). These lines have to be transferred onto the opposite side and here a folding steel rule, with the free

2. Using a mortice gauge to mark the slots

3. Test piece is used to give the precise length of the mortices

ends taped together, is a useful aid. The blades of the rule are sprung apart and the wood inserted, with one blade accurately aligned with the knife line on the face side. A small G cramp is used to hold it in this position, as the marking knife is used to mark the length of the mortice on the underside (photo 4). With this procedure it is unnecessary to make marks on the faces and edges, as the knifed lines are transferred onto the reverse side. The slots connecting the mortice to the outside edge should be marked out initially in pencil then, after checking, cut in with a marking knife to the exact thickness of the test piece. Most of the mortice waste can be removed by drilling, using a twist drill or flat bit, about 1.5mm ($\frac{1}{16}$in) smaller than the mortice width (photo 5). It is better to select a drill small enough to prevent it breaking into an adjacent hole, as happened in the photograph!

The slots can be sawn with the aid of a mitre

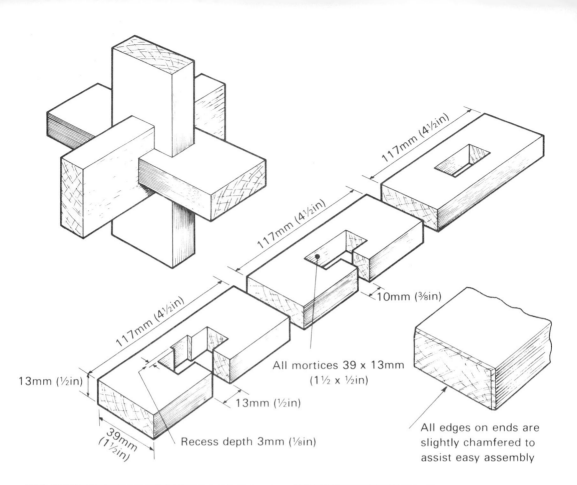

117mm (4½in)

13mm (½in)

10mm (⅜in)

All mortices 39 x 13mm
(1½ x ½in)

13mm (½in)

39mm
(1½in)

Recess depth 3mm (⅛in)

All edges on ends are
slightly chamfered to
assist easy assembly

4. Transferring mortice length onto the reverse
side with the aid of a folding ruler

5. Drilling away the mortice waste

block (photo 6). The wider slot should fit the thickness of the test piece exactly, and can be pared to size if it has been sawn too cautiously. The mortices are chiselled out to size with the wood clamped down onto a piece of waste wood (photo 7). Do not attempt to cut right through

to the opposite side when making finishing cuts near the ends of the mortices. Final cuts should be *exactly* on the marking knife line and executed from each side. *Slight* undercutting of the mortice ends is a worthwhile 'dodge' to obtain well fitting parts. The pieces can be

70

6. Mitre block ensures the squareness of the slots

8. Sawing pieces off to length

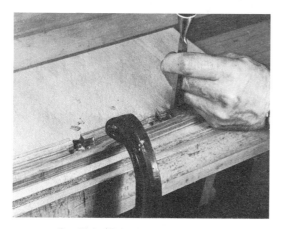

7. Chiselling out mortice waste

9. Planing the ends square on a shooting board

sawn to length on the mitre block (photo 8), and the ends trued accurately, using a disc sander or by planing on a shooting board (photo 9). The plane needs to be really sharp for cutting end grain, and adjusted to remove fine shavings.

To maintain the flatness of the sides and squareness of the edges, the parts should be smoothed by rubbing them against a piece of fine abrasive paper, fixed to a board with double-sided adhesive tape or drawing pins.

Smooth all sides and edges until the pencil lines have been removed, then test for an easy sliding fit. Make adjustments to mortices and slots, if necessary, using a chisel or fine file as required. The edges of all the ends should be chamfered to allow easier alignment and fitting.

Finishing
See chapter 4.

13 Tower of Hanoi

This ancient puzzle will give considerable fun and bafflement to puzzlers of all ages before it can be solved. Manoeuvring the pieces in the required manner is easy initially and most puzzlers are optimistic of an early solution. However, those who try to go too fast soon find that the puzzle becomes more difficult, and eventually the sensible course seems to be to start again . . . In this version the discs are turned to a pleasing and easily handled shape, and the use of different timber species for the discs adds to both the interest and the visual appeal of the puzzle.

Object
The discs are placed on the centre peg with the largest at the bottom, and decreasing in size to the top. The discs must be transferred to an end peg in the same order without at any time placing a larger disc on a smaller one. The other end peg is used as a 'staging post' to effect the transfer.

Construction
Easy. Because inaccuracies do not impair the working of this puzzle it is ideal for the less experienced woodworker. Shaping the discs on a lathe, or with the aid of an electric hand drill, is simple and safe using a scraping tool ground to the edge shape of the discs.

Materials
To give the puzzle 'heirloom' quality the version shown here is made of highly prized Rio rosewood for the base, with pegs of cocobola. The discs are of olive, Indian rosewood, box, padauk, sycamore, teak and yew and were chosen either for their interesting grain or their good colour contrast. The discs present an opportunity to make good use of offcuts of attractive timber too small for most other projects.

Prepared sizes

Base	250 × 80 × 12mm (10 × 3¼ × ½in)
Pegs (3 off)	80 × 10mm (3⅛ × ⅜in) dia. (finished size)
Discs (7 off)	72, 66, 60, 54, 48, 42, 36mm dia. × 8mm thick (2⅞, 2⅝, 2⅜, 2⅛, 1⅞, 1⅝, 1⅜in dia. × ⁵⁄₁₆in thick) (finished size)

Method

Base
The prepared wood for the base should have a centre line pencilled on one side, and the hole centres marked on it. With dividers set to half the width, mark the semicircular ends (photo 1). The waste can be removed with a coping or

1.   Marking the ends of the base with dividers

bandsaw (photo 2), keeping well clear of the line. The sawn edge can be spokeshaved square and true (photo 3) or this can be done with the aid of a disc sander, if available. When sanding the edges smooth, a better result will be obtained if a narrow sanding block is used with the abrasive pinned to it (photo 4). When using a full sized sanding block it is difficult to avoid excessive rounding over of the edges and an imprecise and amateurish appearance can result.

2. Sawing the base ends

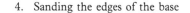

4. Sanding the edges of the base

3. Spokeshaving the ends of the base

If possible, the peg holes should be drilled with a bench drill to ensure that they are truly vertical. It is *possible* to do this by hand, but the help of an assistant is normally necessary to ensure that squareness is maintained in the direction that cannot be sighted. The holes can be made with a twist drill (photo 5) or flat bit. If a twist drill is used, it would be wise to make a 3mm (⅛in) pilot hole first to ensure that the larger drill does not wander off position. If the base is to be covered underneath with baize, the holes can be drilled right through. Otherwise set the depth stop, or take care that they do not penetrate completely. After drilling, the surface of the base can be sanded smooth and the top edges minutely radiused ready for polishing.

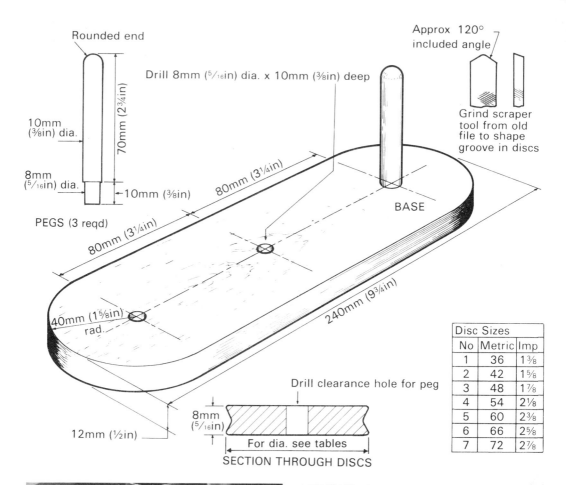

Rounded end

Approx 120° included angle

Grind scraper tool from old file to shape groove in discs

Drill 8mm (⁵⁄₁₆in) dia. x 10mm (³⁄₈in) deep

10mm (³⁄₈in) dia.

70mm (2³⁄₄in)

8mm (⁵⁄₁₆in) dia.

10mm (³⁄₈in)

80mm (3¼in)

BASE

PEGS (3 reqd)

80mm (3¼in)

40mm (1⁵⁄₈in) rad.

240mm (9¾in)

12mm (½in)

8mm (⁵⁄₁₆in)

Drill clearance hole for peg

For dia. see tables

SECTION THROUGH DISCS

Disc Sizes		
No	Metric	Imp
1	36	1³⁄₈
2	42	1⁵⁄₈
3	48	1⁷⁄₈
4	54	2⅛
5	60	2³⁄₈
6	66	2⁵⁄₈
7	72	2⁷⁄₈

5. Drilling the peg holes

6. Sawing out the discs

Discs

The wood for these can be prepared to thickness in the normal way or, if end grain slices are used, as in the puzzle shown here, they can be fixed to the lathe face plate and turned to size. Locate centres on the pieces and mark out the diameters as given on the chart. Set the dividers slightly oversize as the finished diameters will be turned on the lathe. Pilot drill, then drill as for the base, before cutting out well clear of the lines with a coping or bandsaw (photo 6).

The discs can be turned on a wood or metal-

74

7. Shaping the disc edges with form scraping tool

8. Turning the pegs with improvised lathe set up

working lathe or, as shown here, with an electric hand drill (on stand) with a makeshift tool rest. The discs are most easily turned on a threaded mandrel, and a 10mm (⅜in) dia. bolt can be used for this. The threaded portion must be long enough to take the thickness of the wood plus a nut and washer on each side of it. For use in chucks, the head should be sawn off. A bolt can be attached to a woodworking lathe by drilling and counterboring a round piece of wood, preferably thick multi-ply, then fixing this to the face plate. The bolt can be prevented from turning in the wood by driving its head into an undersized counterbore, or by using a carriage bolt with a square shank under its head. Alternatively, a screw chuck could be used and the peg holes drilled after turning.

The edges of the discs can be reduced to the diameters given in the table and checked by callipers. The vee groove is most easily formed with a scraping tool – an old file is ideal – ground to the shape given in the drawing. Take a light cut with the tool (photo 7) and keep it sharp to ensure a good surface finish. Each disc can be sanded smooth and the edges slightly rounded, but care must be taken to see that the abrasive does not foul with the nut or, more painfully, with the fingers!

Pegs
It is impossible to make a puzzle of superior quality using ready-made dowel for the pegs. Its use is tempting – it is, after all, available in the correct diameter – but dowelling is made from the most featureless and insipid wood species, and its use can only detract from the appearance of the finished puzzle.

The effort involved in making the pegs is richly rewarded particularly if an attractively grained wood is used. Sufficient wood should be prepared, at least 4 or 5mm (³⁄₁₆in) oversize, in section, and sawn off about 30mm (1⅛in) over-long. This excess length should be rounded off, using a chisel or rasp, to fit the chuck. The relatively long overhang of the wood from the chuck necessitates a centre to support the free end. On a lathe proper the tailstock centre will, of course, be used; but an improvised set up will require a piece of wood with an imbedded nail arranged to steady the end (photo 8). The turning down can be done with a chisel or simple scraping tool and the end partially rounded, but not severed or the centre support will be lost. Use a small chisel to reduce the end to the spigot diameter and check its size with callipers. The pegs should be sanded in the lathe, then removed to have the centred ends sawn off and the rounding completed. Final smoothing of the pegs should be done length-wise to remove any sanding marks made on the lathe.

Finishing
Polishing and fitting the baize to the underside of the base is dealt with in chapter 4.

14 Travel Solitaire

Perhaps the reason why solitaire retains its fascination is because if you are clever, or lucky, enough to solve it, you are unlikely to remember how you did it. So you try again and again . . . This unique travelling version gives an added dimension to the familiar puzzle by combining contemporary styling with archaic technology. Anachronistic, yet provenly practical, wooden springs are used to control the storage of the steel balls in the hollowed-out base. As each ball is removed, in the course of the game, it is pressed into a hole past a wooden spring, to be retained safely inside until required again. Then, when a button attached to a second wooden spring is pressed, the balls are released to cascade into your hand ready for setting up the puzzle again. The craftsman who enjoys mechanics in wood will find this an unusual and most rewarding puzzle to make. Readers who like to adapt puzzles to their own design should note that a simpler storage chamber shape, for instance a hopper configuration, will not release the balls continuously as required.

Object
The steel balls are placed in all the recesses except the centre one. The balls are removed one by one, after each has been jumped over by another ball. The puzzle is solved when one ball is left in the centre hole. Diagonal moves are not allowed.

Construction
Not difficult – much of the work is concealed inside the base, and the mechanisms will function well even if inexpertly made! The appearance of the puzzle will be much improved if crisp, clean edges can be formed when turning the playing deck and when shaping the outer edge of the puzzle.

Materials
The model shown here is made of plain sycamore with a playing area of tulip wood.

The silky whiteness of the base is a foil on which to display and emphasise the rich colour and striking grain of the tulip wood. The release button is a turned piece of cocobola, and rosewood is used for the springs. Many wood species are suitable for the lightly stressed springs, including beech, box, ash, hickory, yew, etc, and all should perform their function faultlessly for decades.

Prepared sizes

Base	210mm dia. × 19mm (8¼in dia. × ¾in)
Playing deck	140 × 140 × 4mm (5½ × 5½ × ⁵⁄₃₂in)
Ball release and retaining springs	210 × 10 × 3mm (8 × ⅜ × ⅛in)
Ball release button	10mm dia. × 8mm (⅜ dia. × ⁷⁄₁₆in)
Base cover	152mm sq × 0.5mm (6in sq × ¹⁄₃₂in) veneer or thin plywood
Steel balls (32)	11mm (⁷⁄₁₆) dia.

Baize for the underside of the puzzle

Method

As shown in the sequence photographs, the wood used for the base was square and but little larger than the finished size. This meant, when the base was fixed to the lathe faceplate, that the tool cut was an intermittent one. This is unsound turning practice and, particularly for inexperienced woodturners, can be unsafe. It is recommended that the base be turned from a *disc* of wood large enough to accommodate the square base. This does mean, of course, that some wood is wasted, but better and safer results are more easily obtained. Alternatively, it is *possible* to copy the design without using a lathe. The playing deck could be made circular and then glued to the deck, but skill and care would be necessary to get a crisp and accurately sloping surface surrounding the deck.

Base
Mark out a disc of wood 210mm (8¼in) dia. and pencil on two lines through the centre, at

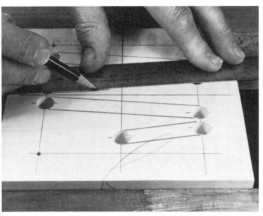

1. Marking the widths of the slots

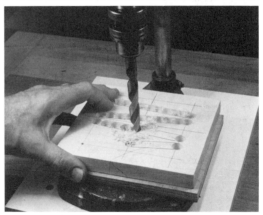

2. Drilling away the waste wood from the slots

right angles to each other. Over these lines construct four 55mm (2³⁄₁₆in) squares. On these squares mark out the positions of the holes at the ends of all the slots, and also the ball entry and button release holes. Centre punch the centres then drill to the sizes and depths shown in the drawing. The widths of the slots can now be marked on with a rule aligned with the edges of the holes, as shown (photo 1). A series of holes can now be chain drilled to remove most of the waste from the slots, using a drill somewhat smaller than the slot width (photo 2). The slots are now pared to the line (photo 3),

then chiselled out to an even depth with the workpiece held in a vice (photo 4). The same procedures can be used to cut the ball retaining spring slot and the sloping recess for the ball release spring. The ball entry and release button holes can now be enlarged from the reverse side – that is the upper surface of the puzzle. All the slots can now be smoothed with abrasive paper wrapped over a small block of wood (photo 5). The ball exit hole is drilled to connect with the short end slot (photo 6). To ensure accurate alignment with the playing deck, and with the lathe face plate, a small hole

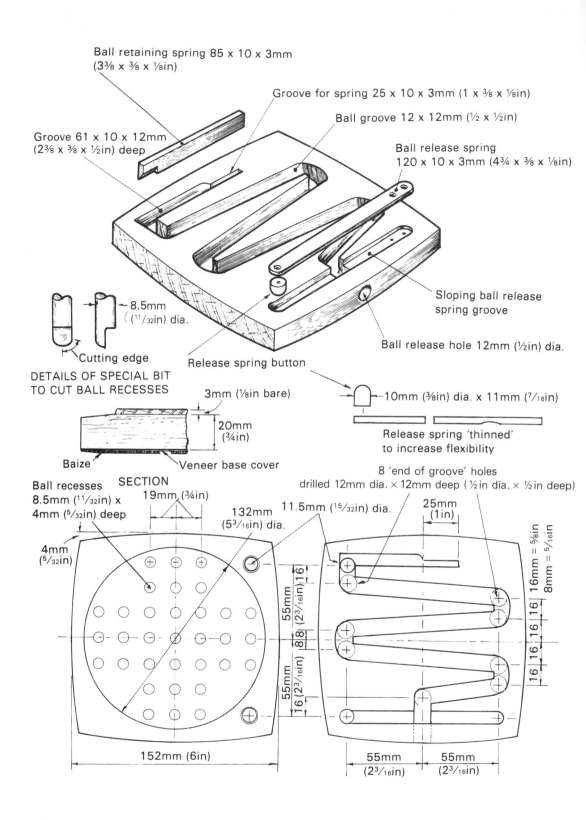

Ball retaining spring 85 x 10 x 3mm
(3⅜ x ⅜ x ⅛in)

Groove for spring 25 x 10 x 3mm (1 x ⅜ x ⅛in)

Ball groove 12 x 12mm (½ x ½in)

Groove 61 x 10 x 12mm
(2⅜ x ⅜ x ½in) deep

Ball release spring
120 x 10 x 3mm (4¾ x ⅜ x ⅛in)

8.5mm
(¹¹/₃₂in) dia.

Sloping ball release
spring groove

Cutting edge

Ball release hole 12mm (½in) dia.

DETAILS OF SPECIAL BIT
TO CUT BALL RECESSES

Release spring button

3mm (⅛in bare)

10mm (⅜in) dia. x 11mm (⁷/₁₆in)

20mm
(¾in)

Baize

Veneer base cover

Release spring 'thinned'
to increase flexibility

Ball recesses
8.5mm (¹¹/₃₂in) x
4mm (⁵/₃₂in) deep

SECTION
19mm (¾in)

132mm
(5³/₁₆in) dia.

11.5mm (¹⁵/₃₂in) dia.

8 'end of groove' holes
drilled 12mm dia. x 12mm deep (½in dia. x ½in deep)

25mm
(1in)

4mm
(⁵/₃₂in)

55mm
(2³/₁₆in)

8|8

55mm
(2³/₁₆in)

16

16mm = ⅝in
8mm = ⁵/₁₆in

16 16 16

16

152mm (6in)

55mm
(2³/₁₆in)

55mm
(2³/₁₆in)

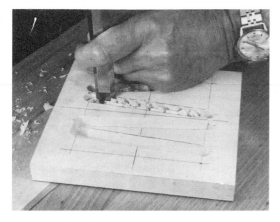

3. Chiselling the sides of the slots

5. Smoothing the slots with abrasive paper wrapped over a block

4. Cleaning out the base of the slots

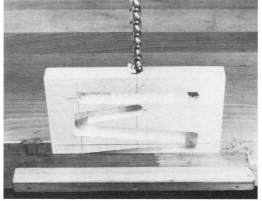

6. Boring the ball exit hole

1.5mm ($\frac{1}{16}$in) should be drilled through in the centre of the base.

Playing deck

Because thin wood sufficiently wide is unlikely to be available in one piece, two or more pieces will require joining together, edge to edge, to make up the width. Their edges should be planed straight and square on a shooting board (see chapter 3), and the abutting edges held together, against the light, to check for accuracy. It is convenient to use vice pressure when gluing the pieces together, supporting them on a slightly narrower piece of wood. Two blocks of wood should be G cramped down onto the playing deck to prevent the thin wood from buckling as the vice is tightened (photo 7). Paper should be used over the supporting wood, and under the blocks, to prevent glue adhering to them. When dry, one side of the deck can be planed or scraped flat and true and

7. Gluing the playing deck edges together

a small hole, identical to that in the base, drilled in its centre.

Assembly

When gluing the playing deck to the base a large or long reach G cramp is useful, in addition to those used near the edges. Discs, of

8. A panel pin is used to align the centres of the base and playing deck

9. Fixing the workpiece to the face plate disc

chipboard or multi-ply, are required on each side of the workpiece to spread the cramp pressure and to ensure the good contact of the glued surfaces. The grain of the playing area should be arranged to be at right angles to that of the base and their centres aligned with a small panel pin (photo 8).

Turning
The usual disc or pad of wood secured to the lathe face for fixing the workpiece should have its centre located. This is easy to do with the lathe running, by pressing a scriber or similar pointed tool against the disc, in a position where it can be held without wobbling. A small hole should be drilled in the centre, and a piece of thin wire used to align the centre of the workpiece with the centre of the face plate disc when they are secured together (photo 9). The playing deck can now be turned to 132mm (5³⁄₁₆in) dia. and the base given the slightly sloping upper surface shape given in the drawing. As shown (photo 10), this is being turned on a square base piece instead of the recommended disc, and great care is required because the tool cut is intermittent. This can be a dangerous practice unless very firm control of the tool is exercised, and the rest is positioned as close as practicable to the workpiece. A light scraping cut over the playing area, checked with a straight-edge, can be used to reduce this to the required 3mm (⅛in bare) thickness. Sanding, too, is a difficult operation on a square base, and only the playing deck and the area of the base immediately adjacent to it should be attempted. The problems mentioned, both of

10. Shaping the playing deck on the lathe

turning and sanding, are eliminated by using a disc of wood for the base.

Shaping
It is convenient to mark out both the outline of the base and the positions of the recesses onto a thin card template. The spacing of the holes is given on the drawing, but the precise diameter of the playing deck should be taken from the workpiece and used on the template. When the outline of the template has been cut out it can be cut into two parts on the circular line. The outer part is placed over the playing deck as the outline is marked (photo 11). Check that the ball entry and button release holes are diagonally equidistant from the corners of the template. The shape of the base can now be sawn with a bandsaw (photo 12) or coping saw, keeping to the waste side of the line. The edges can be trued with a block plane, spokeshave or

11. Marking round a template to give the outer shape of the puzzle

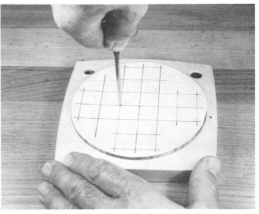

13. Pricking ball recess positions through the template onto the playing deck

12. Sawing the outer edges of the puzzle to shape

14. Drilling the ball recesses

disc sander, then finished with a fine abrasive paper wrapped over a small block of wood.

Ball recesses

The circular part of the template can now be fixed to the playing deck with sellotape or double-sided tape, and the ball recess positions pricked through with a sharp point (photo 13). These recesses can be drilled through with a twist drill, used in a pillar drill, with the depth stop set to allow the holes to just penetrate the playing deck (photo 14). For a superior 'heirloom' appearance a special bit, an adaptation of an engineer's 'D' bit, can be made. This will form shallow hemispherical recesses, and is well worth the short time it takes to make if metalworking lathe facilities are available. It is also practicable to shape it on a grindstone to give a satisfactory result. To make the bit, a short piece of silver steel – or even mild steel – should be shaped to the flat rounded end shape

given in the drawing. Half of the end is then ground or filed away for about 10mm (⅜in). A slightly 'proud' cutting edge is required, and this can most easily be formed by tapping the cutting side of the bit with a pin punch. This will 'spread' the cutting edge slightly and give the necessary clearance. In practice it has not been found necessary to heat treat the bit, but this could be done to a silver steel bit, if preferred. The bit can be used directly to make the recesses, or to finish shallow holes drilled normally.

Ball retaining spring

This should be shaped as shown, and its thickness should make it a tight press fit into its recess. The width of its moving portion can be narrowed, if necessary, to prevent it rubbing against the bottom of its slot or the base, when this is fixed into place. The action of the spring should be tested by pressing balls through its

| 15. Sanding the ball release button | 16. Securing the ball release spring |

entry hole. The sloping edge of the spring can be adjusted by filing, if necessary, and it can be thinned locally, near its recess, if its action is too powerful. A light action should be aimed for, particularly if the puzzle is to be used by young people.

Ball release spring

The button for this can be turned from an offcut of round hardwood held in a drill chuck. After sanding smooth (photo 15) it can be cut to length, and a small hole drilled in its centre to receive the fixing screw. The sloping spring recess, to receive the spring, should be adjusted in depth so that the balls are just held back until the button is depressed. The recess should be somewhat wider than the spring, to allow easy movement, except at its fixed end. Two adjustments to the spring are helpful in achieving the required action. One is to 'thin' the spring locally, close to the second fixing screw, and the other is to use small paper 'shims' under the spring, near either screw, to tilt it slightly in the required direction. Two small countersunk head screws are used to secure the spring in position (photo 16).

Base cover

This can be made of veneer, thin card or aero-modellers' plywood. It should not be glued on in the usual way – the springs may require a 10,000 game service! – but fixed instead with double-sided adhesive tape. This grips firmly and permanently, but will allow the base cover to be levered away in the future, if necessary. The tape should be applied to the base only, and trimmed with a sharply pointed knife so

that it does not overlap any of the slots. When the base cover has been pressed into place its edges can be feathered with a sanding block so that they are invisible from the side. When covered with baize, after polishing, the base cover will be undetectable.

Finishing

Finishing and securing the baize is dealt with in chapter 4.

TRADITIONAL SOLITAIRE

Some readers may prefer to simplify the design given to make a more traditional style solitaire board, as shown in the photograph. This is larger than the travel version but, in the same way, uses a planted-on circle of contrasting wood to delineate the playing area from the base. The base has a circular marble recess, or runnel to use its ancient name, and a similar groove is worked on its edge to give easier lifting and handling. In this instance, the special bit, as detailed in Travel Solitaire for making the ball recesses, but larger, has not penetrated the playing area to give the contrasting hole appearance.

Materials

The puzzle shown is made of Rio rosewood and mahogany, a combination often used in the early nineteenth century when the puzzle was very popular. This is an elegant, rather than exciting, pairing of timbers and more contrasting species can be used if preferred. Being larger than the travel version either steel

balls or coloured glass marbles can be used for the pieces.

Prepared sizes
Overall diameter of the base is 200×20mm ($8 \times \frac{3}{4}$in) thick and the playing deck diameter is 150mm (6in). The recesses are drilled at 20mm ($\frac{25}{32}$in) centres. The glass marbles or steel balls should be 13mm ($\frac{1}{2}$ or $\frac{9}{16}$in) dia., thirty-two required.

15 Tricky Hook

This puzzle, perhaps more accurately described as a trick, was popular up to half a century ago, but is not very well known today. Its modest demands on both time and timber made it a once-popular project for apprentices, who were then fortunate indeed to find a victim not acquainted with the solution! It is, without doubt, a fascinating novelty, and the maker's efforts will be rewarded by the fun and frustration it will afford.

Object
Ostensibly to engage the hook-shaped handle rod onto an elastic loop concealed in the body of the puzzle. As demonstrated, when this is achieved and the handle withdrawn and released, it will fly back with a resounding crack as it impacts against the puzzle body.

Construction
Easy. A problem can be experienced in drilling the hole accurately through the body of the puzzle but a method to obviate this difficulty is detailed in the text.

Materials
The puzzle illustrated is made of Rio rosewood with a dowel of yew. Turning a piece of dowel takes but a few minutes, and it looks far more attractive than the purchased variety.

Prepared sizes
Body and handle   120 × 20mm (4¾ × ¾in) square
Hook and elastic
   dowel   95mm (3¾in) × 8mm (⁵⁄₁₆in) dia.
Small elastic band

Method

Body
Mark off the lengths of the body and the handle (with a small gap between for the saw cut) onto a piece of wood prepared accurately square in section. Saw to length then true up the ends. This can be done on a shooting board with a

finely set plane, against the fence of a disc sander, or with the aid of the cube sanding jig (see chapter 3). Mark diagonals on both ends of the body to locate centres, then check with a pair of dividers (photo 1). Indent accurately

1. Checking centre mark with dividers

with a centre punch or with a nail at each end.

The following procedure may seem somewhat involved for drilling the hole, but in practice, it is all too easy to finish up with it 'off centre', unless precautions are taken. If possible, use a bench drill and grip the body of the puzzle in a machine vice, or clamp it to a

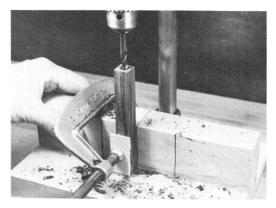

2. Drilling dowel hole through body into handle part

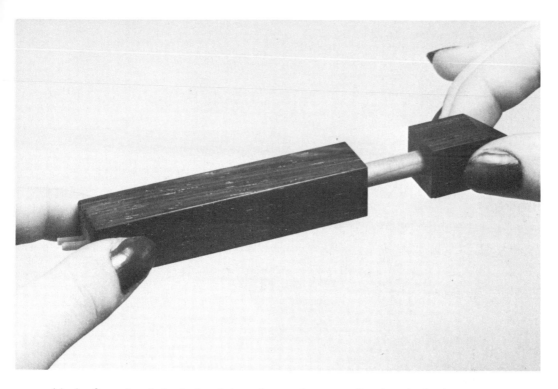

square block of wood and check that it is truly vertical before drilling. The hole should be pilot drilled from each end with a 4mm ($\frac{5}{32}$in) drill to ensure that the larger drill does not wander off position. Next drill through with the dowel sized drill 8mm ($\frac{5}{16}$in) with the body again held accurately vertical. The handle piece can now be secured into place with the body, using sellotape, and, using the same 'set up' to ensure squareness, drill through the body into the handle about 10mm ($\frac{3}{8}$in) deep (photo 2). Separate the parts and drill down into the body with a clearance sized drill, far enough to give an easy sliding fit for the dowel hook.

Dowel hook

Ready-made dowelling is usually made of featureless ramin and its use can only detract from the appearance of the puzzle. Beech dowel is somewhat better but for superior work it is much more satisfactory to turn a piece of contrasting wood to size. Some of the stream-lined tapering of the end can be done on the lathe, but this must not be completed or the centre support will be lost. If a lathe is not available a makeshift arrangement, using an electric hand drill with stand, could be used. When the end shaping has been completed with a tenon saw, a fine saw cut can be made near the

end, to start forming the hook.

Most of the waste can be chiselled away when shaping the hook, taking care not to press too firmly or the wood may be split away (photo 3). A smooth cut three square (triangular) file is ideal for smoothing and truing up the surfaces of the hook notch.

Handle

A spot of glue on the dowel hook will secure it in the handle socket. The tapered end of the handle can now be marked and pared to shape with a chisel (photo 4). The tapers should be

3. Chiselling the hook to shape

85

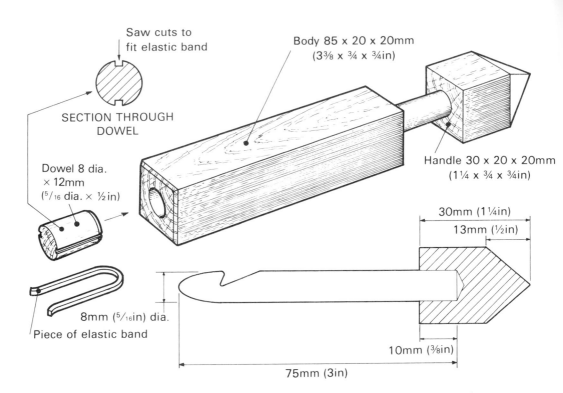

Saw cuts to fit elastic band

SECTION THROUGH DOWEL

Body 85 x 20 x 20mm (3⅜ x ¾ x ¾in)

Handle 30 x 20 x 20mm (1¼ x ¾ x ¾in)

Dowel 8 dia. × 12mm (⁵/₁₆ dia. × ½in)

8mm (⁵/₁₆in) dia.

Piece of elastic band

30mm (1¼in)

13mm (½in)

10mm (⅜in)

75mm (3in)

smoothed by rubbing these surfaces onto a piece of abrasive paper held flat on a board.

A short piece of dowel is used to secure the elastic band into the body of the puzzle. The two small grooves cut into opposite sides are most easily sawn before the dowel is cut to length. The dowel is pressed into position, with the elastic band held over the end, until it is flush with the end of the body. Excess elastic band should be cut away to leave the ends protruding about 8mm (⁵/₁₆in).

Finishing

A heavy build up of wood finish would not suit this rather delicate puzzle so a French (shellac) polish finish is suggested. Three or four coats, applied with a soft brush, should be sufficient and each coat, including the last, should be rubbed down with very fine steel wool. Later, a little wax polish rubbed on will give a pleasing and subdued sheen.

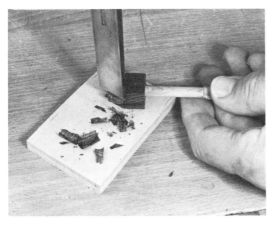

4. Paring tapers on handle end

6
GAMES

1 Bagatelle

Bagatelle, or at least its principle as epitomised in the pinball machine, is still extremely popular today. In amusement arcades and youth clubs it holds its own against the latest electronic video games, albeit by sharing their technology.

This model is far removed from the sophistication of these machines, and also from the primitive early models, with their flimsy plywood sides nailed to the base, and balls propelled into play with a stick. It is a compact, enclosed model in cabinet woods, and is designed to take its place more comfortably in the living room than the playroom. It is an advanced woodwork project incorporating press button flippers, controlled ball ejection and return, and other features that require careful workmanship to ensure that the game will give years of trouble-free operation.

Object

To achieve the highest possible score with the ten balls available. Although undemanding to play, skill does play its part and skilful players can, by controlling the power of their shots and the speed of their reactions in using the flippers, consistently achieve higher scores than 'tug and let go' opponents.

Construction

As presented, it is a challenging project and considerable skill and patience are required to complete it successfully. It will have a special appeal to those who enjoy 'mechanics in wood', involving, as it does, making rather intricate mechanisms and adjusting them to work smoothly and reliably.

However, less experienced woodworkers and those whose time to enjoy their hobby is limited, may like to simplify the design by omitting all, or some, of the elaborate features. Much time could be saved, for instance, if the internal parts were to be left unveneered, while a transparent top is not an essential feature.

Materials

The model shown here is made with a teak case, a playing board of sycamore veneered plywood, and most other parts veneered in Macassar ebony. The flippers are made of Indian ebony and their operating buttons of boxwood. These vital components are made of such dense hardwoods to minimise wear and ensure that they enjoy a long and trouble-free life. The wooden spring to propel the balls is made of beech, though many other woods with the necessary springiness are readily available. Only really hard species should be used for the flippers and operating buttons.

Prepared sizes

Case sides and top end	1200 × 48 × 14mm (47 × 1⅞ × ⁹⁄₁₆in)
Removable lower end	300 × 55 × 14mm (12 × 2⅛ × ⁹⁄₁₆in)
Arch	330 × 190 × 16mm (13 × 7½ × ⅝in)
Flipper assemblies	150 × 65 × 16mm (6 × 2½ × ⅝in)
Playing deck	420 × 280 × 4mm (16½ × 11 × ⁵⁄₃₂in)
Base	420 × 280 × 4mm (16½ × 11 × ⁵⁄₃₂in)
Ball ejection plate	380 × 265 × 4mm (15 × 10½ × ⁵⁄₃₂in)
Ball ejection discs	250mm (10in) × 14mm (⁹⁄₁₆in) dia.
Replay pull strip	430 × 38 × 4mm (17 × 1½ × ⁵⁄₃₂in)
Ball ramp	200 × 16 × 10mm (8 × ⅝ × ⅜in)
Distance piece	75 × 16 × 16mm (3 × ⅝ × ⅝in)
Trigger housing	280 × 25 × 16mm (11 × 1 × ⅝in)
Trigger housing platform	180 × 22 × 13mm (7 × ⅞ × ½in)
Ball guide	250 × 17 × 5mm (10 × ¹¹⁄₁₆ × ³⁄₁₆in)
Inclination block	270 × 20 × 16mm (10¾ × ¾ × ⅝in)
Operating rods	200mm (8in) × 2mm (³⁄₃₂in) dia. brass or steel rod
Operating rod sleeves	30mm (1¼in) × 3mm (⅛in) OD dia. thin wall brass tubing
Flipper pivot pins	40 × 3mm (1½ × ⅛in) brass/stainless steel rod
Operating button return springs (2)	16mm (⅝in) × 6mm (¼in) dia. compression springs

Operating rod	12mm (½in)×3mm (⅛in) dia.
return springs (2)	tension springs
Transparent top (Perspex, Orroglas, etc)	420 × 280 × 3mm (16½ × 11 × ⅛in)
Rub-down numbers	6mm (¼in) high
Balls (10)	11mm (⁷⁄₁₆in) dia. steel balls
Also required:	Off-cut sized pieces of veneer and also hardwood for corner blocks, packing pieces, flippers, trigger operating buttons, wedges, replay pull etc, plus baize and screws

Method

This game consists of a case into which all the component parts are fitted. Because these parts either slide into place, or are fixed by concealed screws, rapid assembling and dismantling is possible. This feature is convenient not only during construction and when applying wood finishes, but in allowing adjustments to be made if required.

Case

Removable end Because access to the inside of the case is made through a removable section of one end, this should be prepared first. The wood has to be cut through lengthwise, and the two pieces then gripped together in the vice with the sawn edges uppermost. These are then planed straight – any lack of edge squareness is unimportant as the error will cancel itself out – and when placed back together again the joint should be all but invisible. If all is well, secure them together with sellotape, and drill and countersink the screw holes. These holes should be a close fit for the screws to ensure accurate alignment of the two pieces. After screwing together, they can be prepared to the same width as the other end and the sides.

Grooves The grooves can be made with a circular saw with a rise and fall table, setting over the fence until the required width of each groove is obtained; or with a plough plane. If a plane is used, a 3mm (⅛in) wide blade will probably be the most suitable for the transparent top panel groove, and may be suitable for the plywood base groove also. The playing deck groove will normally be wider and either a 4mm (⁵⁄₃₂in) or 5mm (³⁄₁₆in) blade can be used. If the groove is too narrow to receive the deck, its edges can be feathered on the underside with a plane until a satisfactory sliding fit is obtained. Note that a playing deck groove is not required in the removable end piece, and that the depth of the base groove should be limited to prevent it fouling the screws.

Radiused edges The upper edges of the case can be planed and sanded to the section given, but

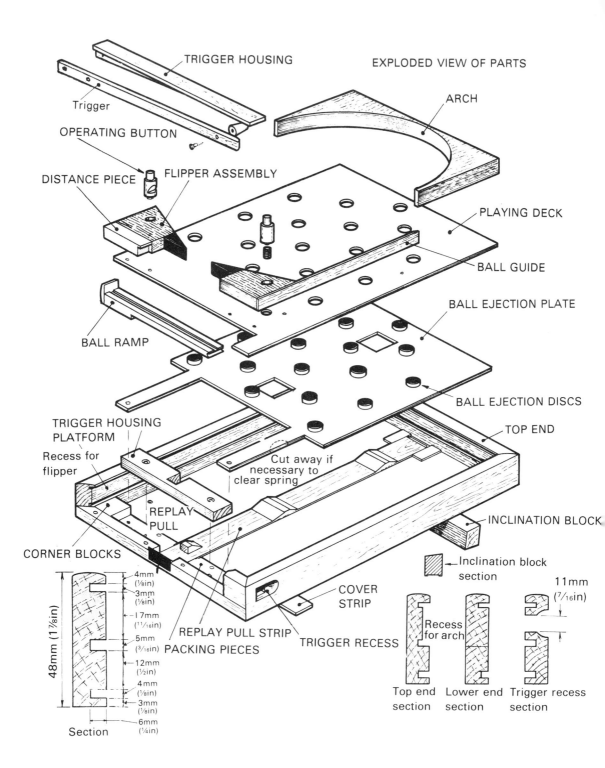

TRIGGER HOUSING

EXPLODED VIEW OF PARTS

Trigger

OPERATING BUTTON

ARCH

DISTANCE PIECE

FLIPPER ASSEMBLY

PLAYING DECK

BALL GUIDE

BALL EJECTION PLATE

BALL RAMP

BALL EJECTION DISCS

TRIGGER HOUSING PLATFORM

Recess for flipper

Cut away if necessary to clear spring

TOP END

REPLAY PULL

INCLINATION BLOCK

CORNER BLOCKS

Inclination block section

11mm (⁷/₁₆in)

4mm (⅛in)
3mm (⅛in)
17mm (¹¹/₁₆in)
5mm (³/₁₆in)
12mm (½in)
4mm (⅛in)
3mm (⅛in)
6mm (¼in)

48mm (1⅞in)

Recess for arch

COVER STRIP

REPLAY PULL STRIP
PACKING PIECES

TRIGGER RECESS

Top end section

Lower end section

Trigger recess section

Section

90

1. Sawing the case corner mitres

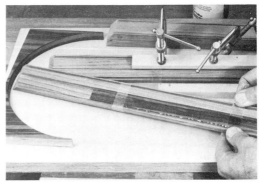

3. Veneering the inside surfaces of the sides

only at this stage if the mitres are to be trued with a disc sander. Otherwise it must be left until after the mitres have been planed on the mitre planing board, because square edges are essential during this operation.

Mitred corners Mark off the internal lengths of the sides and ends, and cut the mitres slightly overlong with the aid of a mitre block (photo 1). The mitres can be trued against the fence of a disc sander or planed on the mitre shooting board (chapter 3). If the latter is used it is necessary to press strips of wood into the grooves to prevent the end grain adjacent to them from splitting. Precise lengths of the sides and ends are not important, but each pair must match accurately. The mitred joints can now be sellotaped together, and the squareness of the case and the fit of the mitres checked.

Arch recesses Shallow housings have to be cut in the end and sides to receive the arch piece. The length of the recess in the sides is one half the inside length of the end, and is measured from the inside edge of the mitre. This can be chiselled out to a depth of 4mm ($^5/_{32}$in), as in

4. Scraping the veneered sides

photo 2. The recess in the end piece is the same depth but extends for its whole length.

Side veneering The visible inside surfaces of the sides are veneered to match the arch and flipper assemblies. After gluing, the strips of veneer should be positioned with sellotape then held down under strips of wood using G cramp pressure (photo 3). When dry, it can be cleaned up with a cabinet scraper (photo 4), then sanded smooth.

Trigger mortice When its position has been marked out, some of the waste can be removed by drilling two 8mm ($^5/_{16}$in) dia. holes close together (photo 5). When the mortice has been chiselled out, the outside finger recess can be gouged to shape (photo 6).

Arch This semi-circular piece is made of thick plywood, or thinner pieces glued together, then veneered on the concave edge and on the upper surface. The plywood should be well oversize initially, and the semi-circle marked out with dividers. The radius marked should be one half the inside length of the end piece. The curve

2. Chiselling the arch recess

91

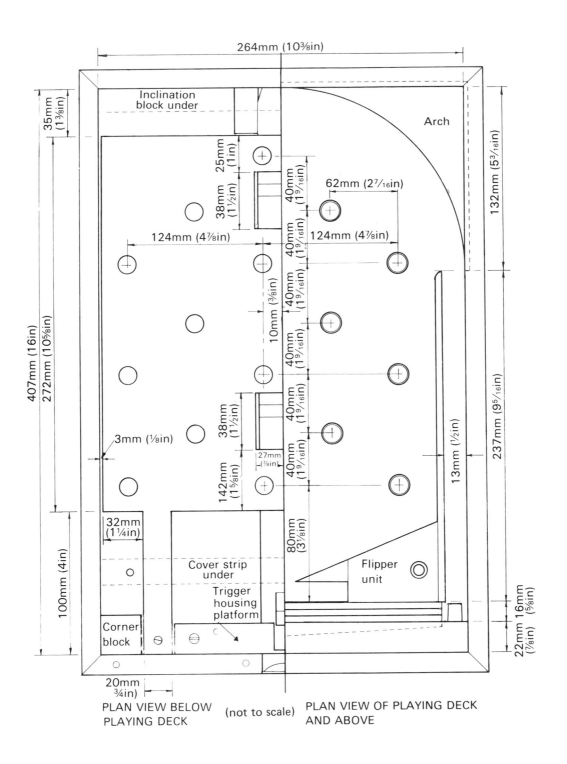

264mm (10⅜in)

35mm (1⅜in)

Inclination block under

Arch

132mm (5³⁄₁₆in)

25mm (1in)

38mm (1½in)

40mm (1⁹⁄₁₆in)

62mm (2⁷⁄₁₆in)

124mm (4⅞in)

40mm (1⁹⁄₁₆in)

124mm (4⅞in)

40mm (1⁹⁄₁₆in)

10mm (³⁄₈in)

40mm (1⁹⁄₁₆in)

407mm (16in)

272mm (10⅝in)

40mm (1⁹⁄₁₆in)

3mm (⅛in)

38mm (1½in)

40mm (1⁹⁄₁₆in)

27mm (⅞in)

40mm (1⁹⁄₁₆in)

142mm (1⅝in)

40mm (1⁹⁄₁₆in)

13mm (½in)

237mm (9⁵⁄₁₆in)

32mm (1¼in)

80mm (3⅛in)

Flipper unit

100mm (4in)

Cover strip under

Trigger housing platform

16mm (⅝in)

Corner block

22mm (⅞in)

20mm ¾in)

PLAN VIEW BELOW PLAYING DECK

(not to scale)

PLAN VIEW OF PLAYING DECK AND ABOVE

92

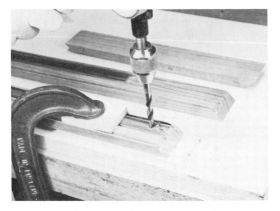

5. Removing some of the trigger mortice waste

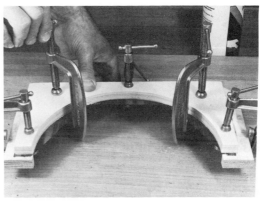

8. Veneering the upper surface of the arch

6. Gouging out the trigger finger recess

can be most easily cut with a bandsaw, and, if done with care, little truing should be necessary before it can be veneered. If cut with a bow or coping saw, the surface can be made square and smooth with a round based spokeshave. If the ends of the semi-circle are cut to terminate in a stop end, considerable pressure can be exerted on the veneer by wedging a thin strip of wood into contact with it (photo 7). The hammer shown in the bottom left-hand corner is driving in a small hardwood wedge against the end of

the strip, to tension it against the veneer. Pressure on the veneer is less good near the ends of the strip, and two G cramps can be applied here to remedy this, plus another in the centre of the curve, if necessary. When dry, excess veneer can be trimmed away and the top and bottom surfaces of the arch sanded smooth. Sufficient offcuts of veneer to cover the top surface should be joined together with tape, then glued down under an arch-shaped piece of wood (photo 8). After cleaning up and sanding the veneered surfaces, the finished size can be marked on and the excess sawn away. The arch now requires careful handling because the narrow central area is somewhat fragile.

Base

For maximum rigidity this should be marked out with the grain across the width, not lengthwise, particularly if 3mm (⅛in) thick plywood is used. It should be an easy fit in the grooves – the inside surface near the edges can be feathered if necessary – and slightly undersized to allow a small gap between its edges and the bottom of the grooves. A too well fitted base could, after gluing, interfere with the close fitting of the mitred corners which is, of course, the more important consideration.

Assembly

The sides and ends should be taped together in a straight line using at least two or three layers of sellotape or vinyl adhesive tape across the mitres. This can then be 'hinged' round into position, complete with arch and base, and the mitres checked. If all is well prepare triangles of plywood ready for using under the arch to align its lower surface with the groove. After any necessary adjustments the joints can be glued, remembering that no glue should be applied to

7. Veneering the inner surface of the arch

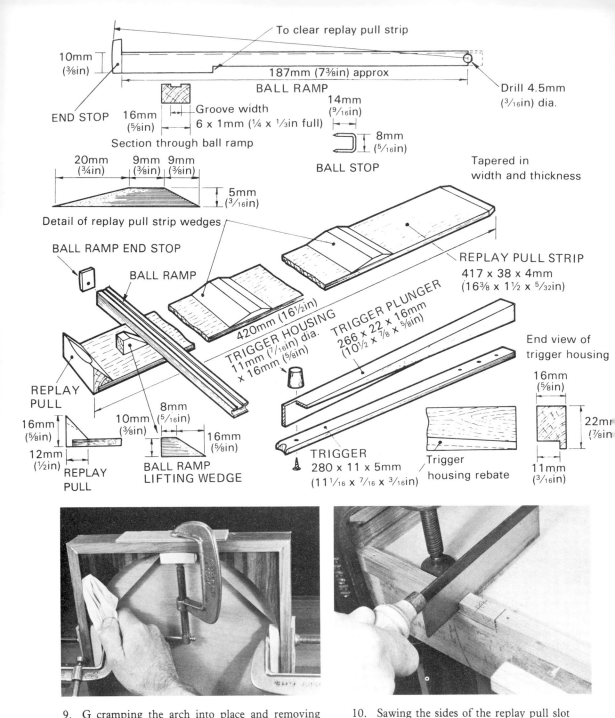

To clear replay pull strip

10mm (³⁄₈in)

END STOP

187mm (7³⁄₈in) approx

BALL RAMP

Drill 4.5mm (³⁄₁₆in) dia.

16mm (⁵⁄₈in)

Groove width
6 x 1mm (¼ x ¹⁄₃in full)

14mm (⁹⁄₁₆in)

8mm (⁵⁄₁₆in)

Section through ball ramp

BALL STOP

Tapered in width and thickness

20mm (¾in) 9mm (³⁄₈in) 9mm (³⁄₈in)

5mm (³⁄₁₆in)

Detail of replay pull strip wedges

BALL RAMP END STOP

BALL RAMP

REPLAY PULL STRIP
417 x 38 x 4mm
(16³⁄₈ x 1½ x ⁵⁄₃₂in)

420mm (16½in)
TRIGGER HOUSING
11mm (⁷⁄₁₆in) dia.
x 16mm (⁵⁄₈in)

TRIGGER PLUNGER
266 x 22 x 16mm
(10½ x ⅞ x ⅝in)

End view of trigger housing

16mm (⁵⁄₈in)

REPLAY PULL

16mm (⁵⁄₈in)

10mm (³⁄₈in)

8mm (⁵⁄₁₆in)

16mm (⁵⁄₈in)

22mm (⅞in)

12mm (½in)
REPLAY PULL

BALL RAMP
LIFTING WEDGE

TRIGGER
280 x 11 x 5mm
(11¹⁄₁₆ x ⁷⁄₁₆ x ³⁄₁₆in)

Trigger housing rebate

11mm (³⁄₁₆in)

9. G cramping the arch into place and removing excess glue

10. Sawing the sides of the replay pull slot

the upper half of the lower end, and then reassembled with a generous amount of tape used to pull the final mitre joint into good contact. After G cramping the arch into place, all surplus glue should be removed with a damp cloth (photo 9), and the triangular ply

alignment pieces removed before the glue sets. After sanding all external surfaces smooth, the removable end piece can be unscrewed and the position of the replay pull slot marked. The sides of this can be sawn (photo 10) and the waste chiselled away to be flush with the upper surface of the base. Two blocks are prepared to size, then glued into the corners to strengthen the mitred corners of the case. Two packing pieces are glued onto the base on each side of the slot, and similar pieces are required near the top end to locate the replay pull strip. The playing deck declivity is given by a block of wood glued to the underside of the base. The section of the block allows a strip of baize to be glued into the shallow groove to provide a non-scratch base.

Replay pull
The small block of hardwood for this should be rebated by sawing and chiselling – its length precludes planing – then glued and secured to its operating strip with a small G cramp. When dry it can be shaped to the section given, and the tapers planed on the end of the operating strip to give self-aligning entry under the ball ejection plate, and between the location blocks, when it is pushed into place.

Playing deck
This can be made most simply from a piece of 4mm ($\frac{5}{32}$in) whitewood birch plywood. This is readily available, and is the correct colour to give contrast with the other parts and the hole numbers, but unfortunately will not give the game 'heirloom' quality. For best effect the deck should be veneered with a white veneer of sycamore, holly or other good quality light coloured wood. The preferred groundwork will be a 'red' 4mm ($\frac{5}{32}$in) plywood with the grain across the width of the board. Suitable veneer for the top surface can often be obtained wide enough in one piece, but, if not, two pieces can be joined edge to edge then secured with tape. The two veneer leaves should be placed together, on a shooting board, and held down flat with a piece of wood as the edges are planed. A perfectly fitting joint should be obtained in this way. A backing veneer is required for the underside of the playing deck, to prevent the warping and buckling that would ensue if only one side was veneered. This veneer can be of any variety, and narrow pieces can be joined together to make up the required width. The veneers should be glued down in a press of which details are given in chapter 3.

When dry, the veneered surface will require cleaning up and, for this, a cabinet scraper is the ideal tool. With one end of the panel clamped down, a sharp scraper will remove fine shavings (photo 11) and the panel will soon be

11.   Scraping the playing deck panel

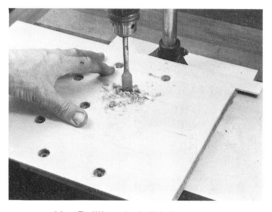

12.   Drilling the ball holes

ready for final smoothing with a fine abrasive used on a cork block. It can then be cut to size and should be an easy, but not sloppy, fit in its groove. If necessary the underside can be slightly reduced in thickness near the edges, until the required fit is obtained. Truing the stopped lower edge of the deck can be done with a bullnosed rebate plane, and a fine file may also be useful in obtaining the required straight edge here.

The hole positions can now be marked with pencil as shown, and also the screw holes for fixing the flipper assemblies and guide strip. The ball holes can be drilled with a sharp flat bit (photo 12), and it is advisable to secure waste wood to the underside of the playing deck during this operation. This will prevent the bit shaking in the holes and avoid consequent damage to them as the bit penetrates the surface and its point guidance is lost.

Ball ejection plate
This is a sheet of plywood with discs attached, which, when it is caused to move upwards,

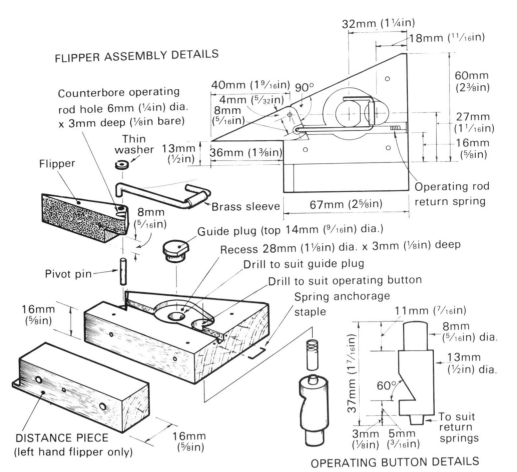

FLIPPER ASSEMBLY DETAILS

Counterbore operating rod hole 6mm (¼in) dia. x 3mm deep (⅛in bare)

32mm (1¼in)

18mm (¹¹/₁₆in)

40mm (1⁹/₁₆in) 90°

4mm (⁵/₃₂in)

8mm (⁵/₁₆in)

60mm (2⅜in)

27mm (1¹/₁₆in)

16mm (⅝in)

Thin washer 13mm (½in)

36mm (1⅜in)

Flipper

Pivot pin

8mm (⁵/₁₆in)

Brass sleeve

67mm (2⅝in)

Operating rod return spring

Guide plug (top 14mm (⁹/₁₆in) dia.)

Recess 28mm (1⅛in) dia. x 3mm (⅛in) deep

Drill to suit guide plug

Drill to suit operating button

Spring anchorage staple

16mm (⅝in)

16mm (⅝in)

DISTANCE PIECE
(left hand flipper only)

11mm (⁷/₁₆in)

8mm (⁵/₁₆in) dia.

13mm (½in) dia.

37mm (1⁷/₁₆in)

60°

3mm (⅛in)   5mm (³/₁₆in)

To suit return springs

OPERATING BUTTON DETAILS

ejects the balls from their holes. After cutting to overall size, the position of the square holes astride its centre line can be marked. Holes can be drilled to remove some of the waste, but a mallet and chisel (photo 13) will, in practice, cut them quickly and effectively. The screw holes drilled in the ends of the 'legs' should be a close fit for the screws. Any slackness here will allow the plate to move, and the close alignment of the ball ejection discs and their holes in the playing deck could be impaired. If the stiffness of the legs hinders the complete upward movement of the plate, they can be 'thinned' locally, in both width and thickness, until sufficient flexibility is obtained.

The replay operating strip can now be fully inserted under the plate, and the prepared wedges glued to it, with their leading (thin) edges just touching the lower side of the square cut-outs. When dry, the action can be tested. As the replay strip is pulled, the ball ejection plate will be lifted by the thickness of the wedges.

13. Cutting the square holes in the ejection plate

With the replay strip removed the playing deck can be slid into position, then the strip replaced to press the ejection plate up and into contact with it. It is now ready to have the ejection discs glued on. If possible, these should be turned to the suggested diameter on a lathe, then parted off to length. The length should be such that

14. Gluing the discs to the ball ejection plate

15. Spreading the glue for the veneered flipper assemblies

each disc protrudes about 0.5mm ($\frac{1}{64}$in full) above the level of the playing deck. Alternatively, the discs could be cut to length from a piece of 16mm ($\frac{5}{8}$in) dia. dowelling thinned down to size. It is convenient to lift and position the discs concentrically inside the playing deck holes by impaling them on the end of a sharp scalpel-like knife (photo 14). When dry, the discs can be smoothed with a fine abrasive and stained black with a felt-tipped marker. Finally, two coats of French (shellac) polish brushed on will give a pleasing sheen to their surface.

Flipper assemblies
These will normally require veneering to match the arch, but a considerable time-saving can be made if solid wood of the same species is available. If not, a piece of firm, well-seasoned hardwood (beech was used in the original) should be prepared for veneering to the sizes given. A piece of the matching veneer is required for the top, and an inexpensive backing one for the underside. When the glue has been spread (photo 15) the veneers can be covered with newspaper and then G cramped down into place (photo 16). When dry, the overlapping veneer can be trimmed away and one edge planed straight and square as a face edge. All marking out should be done from this edge using a marking gauge, a square and a marking knife. The groove should be cut first to a depth of 3mm ($\frac{1}{8}$in) using a circular saw or a plough plane with 4mm ($\frac{3}{16}$in) blade. The hole positions should be indented with a centre punch and, if a large twist drill is to be used for the holes, they should be pilot drilled first with a 3mm ($\frac{1}{8}$in) dia. bit to prevent the large drill wandering off position.

The two large shallow circular recesses can now be cut with a 28mm ($1\frac{1}{8}$in) flat bit until they are level with the base of the groove (photo 17). Check, before drilling, that the large point of the flat bit will not penetrate the upper veneered surface and, if this seems at all possible, shorten the point by filing. The centre

16. G cramps provide pressure for veneering the flipper assemblies

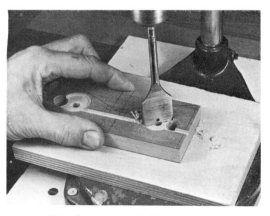

17. Cutting the shallow recesses

18. Drilling the guide plug hole

20. Veneering the sides of the flipper assembly

of the recess is now drilled to receive the guide plug (photo 18) with the depth stop adjusted to limit the depth of the hole. Also drill the flipper pivot pin hole as deep as safely possible, then counterbore (enlarge) it to a depth of 8mm ($\frac{5}{16}$in) with an 8mm ($\frac{5}{16}$in) drill. The two parts can now be sawn to shape and their edges made square and true. This can be done most easily with a disc sander or on a shooting board but, in the latter case, the grooves should be fitted temporarily with strips of wood to prevent the end grain splitting away as they are planed. Some work with the chisel is necessary to connect the operating button holes with the recess, and to form the cavities to receive the flippers (photo 19). The depth of this cavity should be marked on with a gauge, and it should align with the depth of the counterbored flipper pivot hole.

When veneering the edges of the blocks, a shaped clamping pad will be required (photo 20) to ensure that the pressure is applied squarely. As shown, this pad allows two edges to be veneered in one operation. The face edge of the right-hand flipper block, unlike the left-

19. Chiselling the flipper cavity

hand one, requires veneering because its surface is not concealed. When dry, the overlapping veneers can be cut away and the edges sanded smooth. The radiused corners, which allow the flippers to swivel, will not be veneered and the base wood will just be revealed. This is most easily concealed by colouring with a felt-tipped pen to match the veneer.

It is more convenient to shape the stepped ends of the flippers, and drill the required holes, before cutting them to shape. The stepped ends can be sawn and chiselled to shape, then finished with a fine file, if necessary. Each pivot pin hole should be drilled to provide very slight clearance of about 0.1mm for the pin. In practice this means using a 3.1mm drill for 3mm dia. rod and a 3.3mm drill for $\frac{1}{8}$in dia. rod. If it is not possible to drill to these close tolerances, the diameter of the pivot pin can be reduced very slightly, by filing and with an abrasive paper, to give the easy, but not sloppy, fit required. The pivot pins, of brass or stainless steel, can be fixed into place with a smear of epoxy resin. The guide plugs are turned to shape from a piece of firm hardwood and, if they are made a good press fit, it will not be necessary to glue them into place. A flat should be chiselled on the flange facing the operating button hole, to increase the range of movement possible for the operating rod. The double bent end of each operating rod should be made first, and a small file 'nick' will help to give sharp 90° bends as they are tapped round in the vice. A small piece of brass tube sleeving is slipped over the rod before the second bend is made and, if it can be made to rotate smoothly, will usefully reduce friction with the operating button. The parallel return portion of the operating rod should be an easy sliding fit

21. Filing the notch in the flipper operating button

around the guide plug.

The maximum designed movement possible by the operating rod is 6mm (¼in), and the following procedure will ensure that this distance is effectively utilised. Place the flipper in its 'at rest' position, and adjust the brass-sleeved section of the operating rod so that it overlaps the operating button hole by 6mm (¼in). With the rod held in this position, make a scriber mark on it exactly in line with the side of the operating rod hole, nearest the wider end of the flipper. With this mark aligned with the edge of the jaws of a metalworking vice, the free end can be bent to a sharp right angle with a hammer. The excess length should be cut away to leave 5mm (³⁄₁₆in) protruding from the bend.

The operating buttons should be turned, to the sizes given, from a really dense, firm hardwood. A dark wood, na, was originally used for these, then boxwood was substituted to give a better contrast with the Macassar ebony finish of the flipper blocks. The lower spigot should be slightly tapered, to be a good fit for

the compression spring that will be secured there. After most of the tapered recess in the button has been sawn away, it can be trued and smoothed with a threesquare (triangular) file (photo 21). The tapered slot should be just deep enough to allow the flipper to retain its 'at rest' position under the return spring tension given to it via the operating rod. With the flipper assemblies fixed into position on the playing deck, the operating button holes can be drilled through the deck using a bench type drill, if possible, to ensure squareness (photo 22). If the deck is now slid into its groove, the same drill can be used through the operating button holes, to *mark* the position on the base for holes to receive the operating button return springs. The size of drill selected to make these holes in the base should give slight clearance for the diameter of the springs. A thin cover strip of wood glued to the underside of the base converts these holes into sockets to receive the ends of the springs.

The ball guide is made to the sizes given, then glued to the side of the right-hand flipper assembly. When dry it should be held in position and holes located in the playing deck, to allow it to be secured from the underside with small screws. A general underside view of the flipper assemblies, with the ball guide fixed to the right-hand one, is shown in photo 23.

23. General view of flipper units

Ball return ramp
The wood for this should be a dense hard variety which will give a groove with sharply defined edges on which the balls will run freely. This groove can be most easily cut with the aid of a circular saw, but a plough plane may just

22. Drilling the operating button hole through the playing deck

24. Ball ramp in lowered position

25. Ball ramp in raised position

cope with the cutting after a cutting gauge has been used to mark in the width of the groove on each side. A hole, the same diameter as the thickness of the playing deck, is drilled through the ramp where indicated, and this will give a semi-circular pivoting notch when the excess is sawn away. The inside edge of the protruding tab on the playing deck should be rounded with a file, to make a good fit in the ramp notch. The ramp can now be cut to length and its end stop glued and screwed in place. In its lowered position the ramp should be low enough to collect all the balls from the playing deck (photo 24). The ramp is raised by a wedge glued to the replay strip (photo 25), and its position can be found by trial and error. When the wedge has been positioned to raise and lower the ramp fully over its 20mm (¾in) travel it can be glued to the replay strip. The wedge is also the stop, which, when it abuts against the notch in the trigger housing platform, limits the movement of the replay strip and prevents its removal. The trigger housing platform, which is screwed down into position, should allow working clearance for the ramp as it rises and falls.

Trigger arm and housing

The housing conceals a tapered rebate onto which the trigger arm is screwed. The rebate is most easily cut in an overwide block of wood in the usual way, using a circular saw or rebate plane; then wedge-shaped pieces are cut away from both sides to leave the required shape. Alternatively, holes could be drilled to remove much of the waste, then the rebate chiselled out to size. The shaped housing should be cut to length to be a good fit between the sides, and a small cut out made for the trigger plunger. The trigger is a thin strip of springy wood, slightly tapered on its upper edge to prevent friction on the upper surface of the housing. The free end should be slightly hollowed with a half round file or a gouge, to make a comfortable recess for the finger tip. The fixed end is screwed to the housing as shown, and a third screw hole drilled between them for fixing to the left-hand flipper distance piece. A small rectangle of felt or thin rubber should be glued into place to reduce the impact noise of the trigger when it is released. A small tapered plunger, turned from a piece of hardwood, should be screwed to the trigger arm (photo 26) and its function is to retain 'waiting' balls on the ramp as each one is fired. The trigger housing is secured to its platform by two screws which are tightened up from the underside of the base.

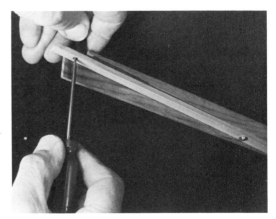

26. Securing the plunger to the trigger arm

Ball stop

The ball stop is bent with pliers, from a piece of brass or stainless steel wire, to the staple-like shape shown. The ends of the legs should be filed to a point and small holes drilled in the side to receive them, or splitting may occur when it is tapped in place. It should be noted

100

that a wooden stop, which may be considered as an attractive alternative, will completely absorb the impact of the ball and the necessary rebound characteristics will be lost.

Plastic top

This can be cut to size with a fine toothed saw and the edges filed smooth. It requires to be a fairly snug fit in the groove, otherwise excessive looseness may interfere with the action of the flipper operating buttons which pass through it. With the plastic panel in position it is possible to peer through it and mark the centres of the button holes. These can be drilled a little undersize initially, and their position corrected with a round file if necessary; then drilled a clearance size for the operating buttons. The holes can then be countersunk to allow maximum operating movement by the buttons. These holes and the countersink can be polished with acrylic or metal polish to remove the 'dulling' effect of the drilling. When inserting the transparent top it will be found that its flexibility allows it to be bowed considerably, and it is not therefore necessary for the flipper operating buttons to be pressed down flush with the flipper blocks.

Finishing

This is dealt with generally in chapter 4. However, peculiar to this project is the strong recommendation that Rustin's clear finish, or similar, should be used for the playing deck. Applied as directed, this can give a most hardwearing and glass-like finish, on which the balls can run freely.

2 Chess Board

Chess players have, over the fifteen hundred or so years that the game has been played, established an almost universal view on what constitutes their preferred chess board. This version should suit both keen players and those who find a board made in distinctive woods an attractive *objet d'art* with which to grace the home. The 50mm (2in) squares suit the popular 75mm (3in) set of chess pieces (King and Queen height), and the playing area is delineated from the surround by narrow banding lines. The international algebraic notation can be included on the surround, and less experienced players will find this a helpful feature when recording or discussing their games.

Unlike the easily damaged veneered edges, usual on manufactured boards, this version uses solid edge lipping which will absorb impact without much ill effect. It also allows a rebated or a moulded edge treatment to be incorporated if desired. Staunton boxwood chess men, with felted and weighted bases, are the recommended pieces to use with this board. Inevitably these are expensive, but a very acceptable alternative set, in hard plastic, can be obtained from specialist suppliers at modest cost.

Object

It is beyond the scope of this book even to encapsulate the basic aims of the game, except to say that each player aims to checkmate the opponent's King. Perhaps its complexity, and the fact that much of its theory is revised and refuted so frequently, accounts for the fact that more books are published on chess, worldwide, than on any other subject!

Construction

Using the procedures described here, which will ensure that the squares are accurately cut, most craftsmen should achieve pleasing results. A veneer press is essential to ensure the successful gluing down of the veneered playing surface. Details of this are given in chapter 3.

Materials

Sycamore is the traditional, readily available, veneer species to use for the 'white' squares, although several other pale varieties are equally pleasing. The choice for the 'black' squares is wider and includes Indian and Rio rosewood, walnut, teak, etc. The board illustrated is made with satinwood and Macassar ebony squares, a most attractive combination, but the latter is not always suitable as some veneer leaves have rather wide and distracting light coloured streaks alternating with the dark wood. The border around the playing area is veneered in the same wood as that used to lip the block-board base wood. This gives the appearance, at least to the uninitiated, that the squares are inlaid in a base of solid wood.

Prepared sizes

Baseboard	430mm square × 16 or 19mm (17¼in square × ⅝ or ¾in) laminboard, blockboard, or chipboard
Lippings	1900 × 18mm or 21 × 16mm (76 × ¾in or ⅞ × ⅝in)
Veneer border pieces (4)	475 × 25mm (19 × 1in)
'white' square pieces (4)	475 × 50mm (19 × 2in)
'black' square pieces (4)	475 × 50mm (19 × 2in)
Lines (strings)	
White pieces (4)	420 × 3mm (16¾ × ⅛in)
Black pieces (4)	420 × 3mm (16¾ × ⅛in)
Backing veneer	470mm (18¾in) square
Rub-down letters and numbers	10mm (⅜in) size

Method

Board

The material for this should be prepared to 430mm (17¼in) square. Exact size is not important, but it should be accurately square or the mitred corners of the veneered surface will not coincide with those of the base. Hardwood lipping pieces are glued to the edges of the base and, if possible, should be of the same species as

Peter, three times British Junior Chess Champion, uses the board described here to analyse a chess position

the veneer border strips. The ends of lipping pieces can be sawn on a mitre block then fitted into place around the base board. If any adjustments are necessary, the ends can be planed on a mitre shooting board (photo 1) or sanded on a disc sander with mitre fence attachment (see chapter 3). If a lipping piece is cut, or trimmed, to be too short it can be lengthened, in effect, by planing its inner surface. The lipping pieces can be glued and held in place by sash cramps or, as shown here,

by small edging cramps (photo 2).

When dry, the overwide lippings have to be reduced to be flush with the surface of the board. As shown (photo 3), the planing should be done with most of the sole of the plane in good contact with the board to ensure that the edges are not reduced in thickness. The entire surface, on both sides, should be well flattened with a medium grit abrasive paper, used on a cork block, to prepare the surface for gluing.

103

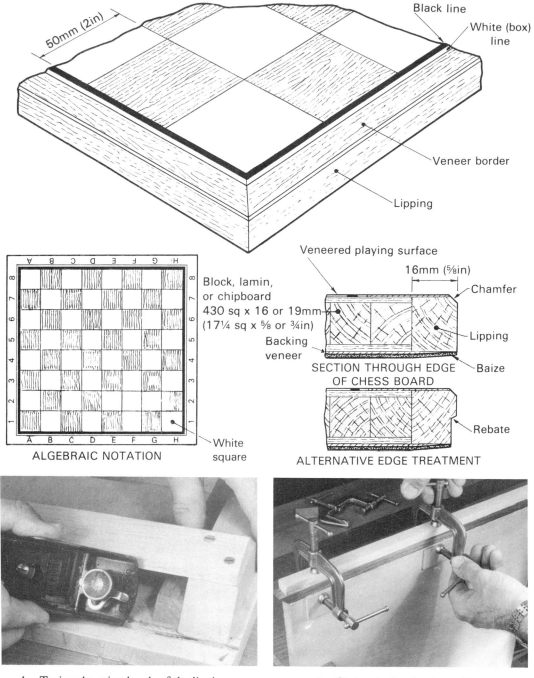

50mm (2in)

Black line

White (box) line

Veneer border

Lipping

Veneered playing surface

16mm (⅝in)

Chamfer

Block, lamin, or chipboard
430 sq x 16 or 19mm
(17¼ sq x ⅝ or ¾in)

Lipping

Backing veneer

SECTION THROUGH EDGE
OF CHESS BOARD

Baize

ALGEBRAIC NOTATION

White square

Rebate

ALTERNATIVE EDGE TREATMENT

1. Truing the mitred ends of the lipping

2. Gluing the lipping in position

The squares

Most of the familiar problems associated with cutting squares of veneer accurately to size for chess boards can be eliminated with the aid of a 50mm (2in) wide parallel straight edge. This is available from metal stockists (see the Yellow Pages) in the form of gauge plate, which is high quality steel, accurately parallel, and 3mm (⅛in) thickness is ideal for this purpose. Less expensive, and often equally suitable, is B.D.M.S. (Bright Drawn Mild Steel), but the edges should be checked to see that they are straight and have not been damaged in any way.

The veneer for the squares – sufficient for

3. Planing the lipping flush with the base board

5. Taping the veneer strips together

4. Cutting the veneer strips to width

6. Cutting off the squares across the grain

four light and four dark strips – should be cut off about 475mm (19in) long. The straight edge is held down very firmly over the veneer and a really sharp hobby or scalpel type knife used to cut along *both* edges of the straight edge (photo 4). The handle of the knife should be inclined slightly away from the vertical position to compensate for the tapered end of the blade. The cutting should always be made over a board of plywood or hardboard, never chipboard. The latter contains many abrasive and glue particles and the cutting edge of the blade would soon be rendered useless. If difficulty is experienced in holding the straight edge down, without movement between the cuts, it can be fixed in place with a few short pieces of double-sided adhesive tape.

The strips of veneer, in alternate colours, can now be secured to each other with short strips of sellotape used to pull the edges together in good contact (photo 5). All the joints between the veneers should now be covered lengthwise with pieces of thin brown gummed paper. This is supplied by veneer stockists and is used to prevent glue penetrating through the joint

when it is glued down under pressure. Strips of chequered veneer now have to be cut off across the grain *exactly* at right angles to the assembled strips. This is not so easy to accomplish, particularly if hard or brittle veneer species are used. It is helpful, therefore, if the straight edge is held firmly in place by a G cramp after its squareness with the edge has been checked with a large set square or the edges of a sheet of A4 paper (photo 6). When cutting across the grain, several firm strokes with the knife should be made but they should stop short of the complete width. The uncut portion should be tackled from the opposite end, thereby preventing the splitting away of the veneer which would undoubtedly occur if the knife was used across the width in one direction only. As before, the cuts must be made on *both* edges of the straight edge and this necessitates wasting 2 or 3mm ($\frac{1}{16} \times \frac{1}{8}$in) between each strip of chequered veneer. It is prudent to check the squareness of the straight edge each time it is cramped down in a new position. In this way no error can creep in, as would be possible if the parallelism of the wastepiece between each strip

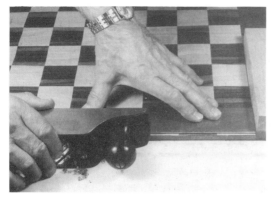

7. Planing the newly assembled edge straight

8. Mitring the corners of the border veneer

was estimated by eye. When each alternate chequered strip has been turned end for end, they can be secured together in close contact and, hopefully, in perfect alignment, using short strips of sellotape. As before, the joints should now be covered on the front surface with the brown adhesive tape. It is worthwhile planing along the recently formed long edges, with the grain, to remove any imperfections of alignment. This should be done on the shooting board, with the chequered surface held down flat with the straight edge (photo 7). A clearer view of the planing is given if the taped side of the veneered surface is placed underneath.

Border
Strips of veneer for this should be cut off with the knife and straight edge. A pair of strings, narrow precut pieces of veneer in contrasting colours, are fixed to one edge of each border strip with small pieces of sellotape. The tape should be applied to pull the strings tightly together and into close contact with the border strip. Any tape which overlaps should be cut away, or it could fold over and interfere with the close fitting of the edge joints. The ends of the border strip now have to be cut to 45° to form the mitres where they meet in the corners. A thin metal template, cut to an angle of 135°, is useful for this, as shown (photo 8). It is convenient to cut, fit and secure the border strips to the *underside* of the chequered surface with sellotape. Then, when the joints have been securely taped on the other side, the pieces of sellotape can be peeled away to give a clear surface for gluing. The tips of corners can be trimmed away with scissors, if necessary, to allow easier sighting of the mitres when aligning them with those on the base.

Veneering
It is necessary to glue a backing veneer to the underside of the board to balance out uneven tensions that are induced if only one side is veneered. The backing veneer, usually an inexpensive variety, can be made from offcut widths taped together. It can be glued on at the same time as the chequered veneer, or separately. Speed is essential when gluing the veneered surface down, and the preparation should ensure that all the necessary equipment is to hand before starting. An arrow, marked on the base board (unnecessary for chipboard, of course) will indicate the direction of the grain, which may be obscured by the layer of glue, and serves as a reminder that the grain of the veneer panel *must* be laid at 'right angles' to it. A notched spreader is a useful aid to ensure that the glue is spread rapidly and evenly over the surface (photo 9). The sheet of veneered squares can now be placed on the baseboard with the mitred corners of each accurately aligned. It can be secured with several strips of sellotape to

9. Spreading the glue on the base board

106

10. Tightening down the veneer press nuts

11. Using a cabinet scraper to clean up the top

ensure that it does not slide out of position when the veneer press is tightened down. The veneered surface should be covered with several sheets of newspaper before the press is tightened (photo 10). The veneering press, and details of the procedures, are covered more fully in chapter 3.

When removed from the press, the criss-crossing layers of tape on the surface of the board can be loosened, and much of it removed by rubbing with a damp cloth. The surface can then be made smooth and true with a cabinet scraper, with the board G cramped down to the bench (photo 11). Similar results can be obtained using a medium grit abrasive paper over a cork block. Final smoothing should be with a fine abrasive paper which can also be used carefully around the border, following the grain. Any overlapping veneer can be cut away with the knife, and the edges planed. The upper edge can be planed to give a small chamfer, or a slight decorative rebate could be worked onto the edge. This has the advantage of making a heavy board easier to lift. The edges of the backing veneer can be sanded away so that it cannot be seen from the sides.

Finishing
This is dealt with generally in chapter 4. If the letters and numbers giving the algebraic notation are used this should be done after two sealing coats of finish have been applied. It is essential that the notation is applied with H1 indicating 'whites' right-hand *white* square. Further coats can then be added to build up a fully protective surface and to seal them in place. Some rub-down letters are dissolved by certain finishes, but most seem to be unaffected by French (shellac) polish and this can be used to seal the letters in before other finishes are applied. It is wise to test the letters and the finish for any reaction before they are used on the board. Letraset numbers and letters seem immune to the solvent effect of most finishes and, if available, are recommended as the best ones to use.

3 Chinese Chequers

This relatively modern game is thought to have appeared first in the USA in the 1930s, and is usually considered to be a development of the nineteenth century game 'Halma'. It is a popular 'adversarial' board game, easier than chess and comparable in difficulty with draughts, and can be played by two to six players.

The layout of the playing area lends itself particularly well to veneering in different woods and, if these are chosen carefully, a very striking and attractive board can be made. Further impact is given to the game by the sets of coloured glass marbles, and the contrasting colour of the recesses to receive them.

Object

The winner is the first player to get all his marbles into the triangle, or star point, opposite his own. If two are playing, each has fifteen marbles of one colour in the triangle which is in front of him and opposite his opponent's triangle. If three or more are playing, each player has ten marbles of the same colour, instead of fifteen. These marbles can be placed within any triangle of the player's choice. Turns are decided in the usual way, then each player moves his marble forward across the board one space at a time unless a jump is possible. A player may jump any marble, either his own or his opponent's, providing the hole beyond is open. Multiple jumps can be made when several marbles are placed in alternate positions with open holes. A player may not move backwards except in a series of multiple jumps which end ahead of the marble's starting point.

Construction

Relatively easy. Care and accuracy are necessary when cutting the veneer shapes and their lines but, given their modest size, they can be readily and economically re-cut if spoilt.

Materials

The example shown is made with a board of solid mahogany, with the central hexagon veneered in bird's eye maple. The 'base' triangles are veneered with satinwood, plain and fiddleback sycamore, Macassar ebony, Rio rosewood and padauk. Black and box lines encompass and delineate the separate veneered areas, and the fill-in surround is veneered in mahogany to match the base. It gives a better appearance if the solid base board, or its edging strips, match the fill-in surround veneer. The top then presents the appearance, at least superficially, of being inlaid rather than veneered.

The relatively large playing area can be made successfully from a single piece of solid timber, or from two or more pieces joined edge to edge provided the wood is known to be well seasoned. Solid wood has several advantages over man-made boards; it does not require edge lipping (a considerable saving in time when a hexagonal shape is involved) and the marble recesses present a much better appearance when they penetrate the veneer. If suitable solid wood is not available, three layers of 6mm (¼in) thick hardboard, glued together, will give a reliable if somewhat heavy board material. Ideally, it will require edge lipping, but it is stable and the recesses will not be unattractive. If other man-made boards are used, a better appearance can be given to the recesses by using a flat or forstner bit, and lining the holes with discs of baize.

Prepared sizes (approx)

Base board	380mm sq × 20mm (14⅜in sq × ¾in)
Surround veneer (6)	200 × 85mm (8 × 3¼in)
Hexagon veneer	230 × 200mm (9 × 8in)
Triangle veneers of different species (6)	120mm sq (4½in sq)
Lines (box)	1500 × 3mm (60 × ⅛in)
Lines (black)	750 × 3mm (30 × ⅛in)

Method

Base board

This should be prepared oversize in both length and width, from solid hardwood or from

laminated hardboard as mentioned above. If hardboard is used the layers should be glued together in the veneer press (see chapter 3).

Templates

Two templates, one hexagonal and one triangular, are essential to ensure the accurate cutting out of the veneer pieces. They can be made from thin aluminium or tinplate or, if these materials are not readily available, from thin plastic such as acrylic sheet or melamine laminate. The easiest and most accurate method to use for marking out the hexagon is to enscribe a circle with a sharp pair of dividers set at 100mm (3¾in), then step off this radius into the circumference to give six equal divisions. Before altering the setting on the dividers also mark the corner positions of the triangle. These marks can now be connected with a rule and scriber to give the hexagonal and the triangular shapes. The marble recess centres should now be accurately marked onto the triangular template. These positions should be centre punched, then drilled about 1.5mm (¹/₁₆in) dia. If a small drill is not available, the centres can be pierced with a sharp point tapped through onto a wood block. The underside of the template should be smoothed with a file to remove punch or drill burrs from around the holes.

If inlaid lines are to be used to delineate the various parts of the playing deck, and to give an attractive edging for the triangles, it is now necessary to *reduce* the size of each template all round by *half* the width of the 'line'. In the game shown the veneer 'lines' are 3mm (⅛in) wide, and therefore borders 1.5mm (¹/₁₆in) wide were marked *inside* the hexagon and triangle templates. They can now be cut out with tinsnips just clear of the border lines, then the edge smoothed and made true with a sharp smoothcut file.

Cutting the veneers

The hexagonal template should now be placed over a suitable piece of veneer, and the shape

1. Cutting along the sides of the hexagonal template.

109

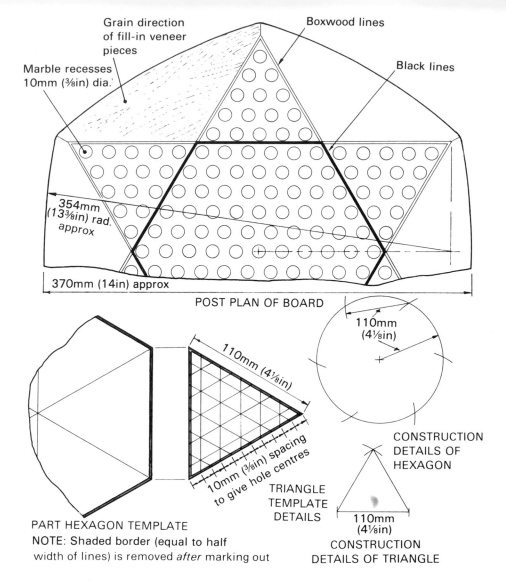

Grain direction of fill-in veneer pieces

Boxwood lines

Marble recesses 10mm (3/8in) dia.

Black lines

354mm (13 3/8in) rad. approx

370mm (14in) approx

POST PLAN OF BOARD

110mm (4 1/8in)

110mm (4 1/8in)

10mm (3/8in) spacing to give hole centres

CONSTRUCTION DETAILS OF HEXAGON

TRIANGLE TEMPLATE DETAILS

PART HEXAGON TEMPLATE
NOTE: Shaded border (equal to half width of lines) is removed *after* marking out

110mm (4 1/8in)

CONSTRUCTION DETAILS OF TRIANGLE

cut out with a really sharp marking or hobby type knife (photo 1). A better appearance is given to the board if the veneer for this has an indeterminate grain direction, and for this reason bird's eye maple was chosen for the original. It may be helpful to secure the template to the veneer with small pieces of double-sided adhesive tape, to prevent the possibility of movement between them. This has the advantage, also, that knife cuts can be made in either direction around the template, without the risk of altering its position. Cutting must be done over a wood or plywood surface (photo 2), and never onto chipboard, which would quickly remove the fine cutting edge of the knife. One corner of the triangular pieces of veneer will be quite fragile, due to the short grain at that

2. Cutting the triangle pieces

point. This problem, dependent to some extent on the species of veneer, can be prevented by fixing sellotape over the corner area before cutting out.

3. Mitring the ends of the lines

5. Aligning the rule with the edge of the triangle

4. Attaching the triangles to the hexagon

6. Cutting the fill-in veneer to size

Lines can now be attached to the edges of the hexagon with sellotape, mitring their corners where they meet. The angle of the mitre is given by aligning the rule with the centre of the hexagon as the knife cut is made (photo 3). When attaching the contrasting lines to the veneer triangles they should *not* be secured to the edge which is parallel to the grain. This will facilitate the sanding smooth of the top, because the grain of the triangles will be more nearly aligned with the fill-in veneer pieces between them. The lines are mitred where they meet at one corner of the triangle, but at the other two corners they are trimmed to be flush with the edge.

The triangles can now be attached to each side of the hexagon, with sellotape tensioned across the joints to pull them tightly together (photo 4). As shown, this tension causes the triangles to rise up, but when the veneer fill-in pieces are fixed betwen them they will then be held flat. Each fill-in piece of veneer, of the same wood species as the base board if possible, should be cut well oversize initially, and its left

7. Mitring the ends of the fill-in pieces

hand edge then attached to one side of the triangle with sellotape. The excess length of the veneer should be fitted under the adjacent triangle, and a rule held against its edge or, more precisely, its line (photo 5). If the triangle is now hinged inwards, the knife can be used against the rule to cut the second edge of the fill-in veneer. When the triangle is hinged back

111

it should make a perfect fit against the cut edge of the fill-in veneer (photo 6). The ends of the fill-in pieces are mitred where they meet against a rule aligned with the triangle corner and the centre of the hexagon (photo 7). All joints should now be covered with thin brown gummed paper to prevent glue penetrating through them when the veneer is glued down under pressure.

Veneering
The press shown here is using four bearers, but, if several G cramps are available to apply pressure near the ends, just two will be sufficient (see chapter 3). The glue should be spread evenly over the base board (photo 8), then the veneered sheet fixed to it with tape to prevent it sliding out of place when the press is tightened. After covering the veneer with several sheets of newspaper the press can be tightened down. It is important that the press is not overtightened, particularly when the workpiece being veneered is smaller than the size of the cauls, as this can *reduce* the pressure in the centre of the press. Such problems can be avoided by checking the flatness of the top caul with a straightedge adjacent to each bearer as the nuts are tightened (photo 9).

Cleaning up
Much of the tape on the veneered surface can be removed with a damp cloth which should be firmly rubbed over the surface (photo 10). When dry, the board can be cramped down to the bench and the surface cleaned up with a cabinet scraper (photo 11). Alternatively the surface can be rubbed flat with medium grit abrasive paper used on a cork block, then finished with a fine abrasive.

Shaping the board
The curved edges of the board can be marked with a pencil, used against the end of a thin batten pivoting on a panel pin (photo 12). The position for the pin is given, as shown in the drawing, by the intersection of two lines. One connects the points of the triangles, and the other line passes through the opposite corners of the hexagon. The pin is not, of course, driven into the veneered surface, but just held gently against it or onto a scrap piece of card. The edges can be shaped most easily with a bandsaw (photo 13) or, because the curve is slight, cut with a circular or handsaw. The edges can be smoothed and trued with a block plane (photo 14) and the corners rounded with a

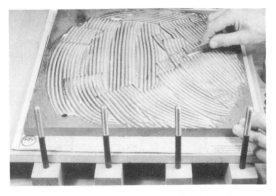

8. Spreading the glue on the base board

9. Checking the flatness of the top caul

10. Using a damp cloth to remove tape

spokeshave. A small rebate can be worked onto the edges of a solid hardwood base board. It also allows the board to be lifted more readily. It *can* be cut using a rebate plane with fence, but this is not easy because the edges are curved. The original was cut on a circular saw, with the blade protruding about 9mm (⅜in) above the table, and tight against a wood surfaced fence. This does not give a very good finish, but the rebate can be smoothed and its step slightly bevelled with a small rebate plane (photo 15).

11. Smoothing the top with a cabinet scraper

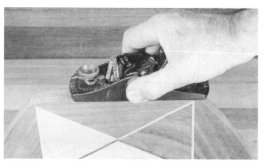

14. Planing the curved edges

12. Marking the curved edges

15. Bevelling the rebated edge step

13. Sawing the edges to shape

16. Drilling the marble recesses with a special bit

Marble recesses

The positions of the marble recesses – all 191 of them! – can be pricked through the triangular template onto the playing surface, with a sharp point. These marks should now be interconnected, in all directions, by pencil lines. This may seem like a reversal of usual procedures – such lines usually *locate* the hole centres – but they are necessary to check the correct positioning of the special marble recessing bit. This bit, details of which are given in chapter 5 (Travel Solitaire), does not have a point which can be accurately aligned with the marked centres. Instead, the bit is just touched onto the work, then lifted, and its mark can then be inspected

in relation to the radial pencil lines. If it is not central to them, the workpiece can be moved slightly to correct the deviation. The depth stop on the pillar drill should be set to give an equal depth for all the recesses (photo 16). The surface should be smoothed with a fine abrasive paper to remove the pencil lines and any burr from around the holes. As far as practicable, the final smoothing should be done *with* the grain of the individual pieces.

Finishing

This is dealt with in chapter 4. The underside of the board could be covered either with baize or with discs of the board material secured near each 'corner'.

4 Labyrintspel

This fascinating game was invented by Sven Bergling in Sweden and was first produced commercially in 1946. Since then over 2 million have been exported to over fifty countries and, in spite of competition from sophisticated electronic games, over 125,000 are still manufactured and sold each year. That the game is so little altered from its original concept is a tribute to its inventor who 'got it right' some forty years ago. Steadiness, patience, confidence, anticipation and speed of reaction are all tested by this compelling machine. Its appeal is wide and few can resist the challenge. Unusually, success, or otherwise, is quite independent of intellect or age. All compete on equal terms – player against mindless ball!

The production model is an example of straightforward functional design executed in economical and serviceable materials. This hand-crafted version differs little in principle from the original, but being a 'one off' game and freed from commercial considerations, it can be made in cabinet woods and incorporate refinements of detail and design. Carefully made and finished, this game will be a treasured family heirloom certain to provide fun and frustration for many generations to come.

Object
To manoeuvre the steel ball past some forty unguarded holes on its course from start to finish. The ball is made to roll by tilting the playing deck, using the two control knobs. The hazard holes are numbered to enable you to compete against friends, or yourself, in achieving and recording as high a score as possible.

Construction
Although not a suitable project for the inexperienced woodworker, the use of a mitre planing jig can, nevertheless, greatly simplify the fitting of the corner joints. Patience, rather than skill, is required when making and fitting the somewhat fiddly barriers to the playing deck. It is a most interesting and worthwhile project.

Materials
The game shown in the photograph is made mainly of teak, with a sycamore veneered plywood deck and Macassar ebony barriers. These woods contrast well with each other and give pleasing visual impact. Almost any hardwood, or indeed a softwood as used in the production models, can be used for the case and frames, and if a piece of whitewood ply (birch) is used for the playing deck, the veneering of it would be unnecessary.

Prepared sizes

Carcase	1270 × 90 × 10mm (50 × 3½ × ⅜in)
Inner frame	1200 × 22 × 7mm (47 × ⅞ × ¼in)
Playing deck frame	1100 × 22 × 7mm (43 × ⅞ × ¼in)
Playing deck	290 × 240 × 4mm (11½ × 9½ × ⁵⁄₃₂in) plywood
Barriers	1520 × 8 × 6mm (60 × ⁵⁄₁₆ × ⁷⁄₃₂in)
Base	310 × 265 × 4mm (12¼ × 10⅜ × ⁵⁄₃₂in) plywood
Grooved base holder	270 × 30 × 8mm (10½ × 1³⁄₁₆ × ⁵⁄₁₆in)
Base end piece and base stop	270 × 40 × 6mm (10½ × 1⁹⁄₁₆ × ¼in)
Spindle blocks	140 × 16 × 8mm (5½ × ⅝ × ⁵⁄₁₆in)
Ball holder rod	115 × 3mm dia.(4½ × ⅛in dia.) stainless steel or brass
Spindles	650 × 6mm dia.(26 × ¼in dia.) brass or mild steel rod
Also required:	6mm (¼in) rub-down numbers and letters, 2 operating knobs, 2 tension springs, nylon or terylene cord, screws and screw eyes, vinyl tape, 3 and 6mm (⅛ and ¼in) brass washers, 14mm (⁹⁄₁₆in) dia. steel ball

Method

Carcase
The lengths of the sides and ends should be marked onto the prepared wood, then sawn off

114

start

finish

1. Planing the ends of the carcase pieces on a shooting board

2. Mitring the ends on a mitre shooting board

slightly overlong. The end grain can be trued to accurate squareness and length, using a disc sander or by planing on a shooting board (photo 1). Precise length is not too important but each pair of pieces should be identical. The ends can now be mitred on the disc sander with tilting table, or with the aid of a mitre shooting board (photo 2), see chapter 3. Either method will produce accurate mitred corners which would be impossible to achieve solely by hand control of the plane. When the ends have been mitred, the pieces can be placed flat on a bench, end to end, and the joints taped across as shown (photo

3). Sellotape or vinyl tape are suitable and two or three layers will usefully increase the pressure on the joints when they are hinged together. If teak is used, as in the original, it is necessary to de-grease both the joints and the area to be taped with methylated spirit (wood alcohol), trichloreothane, or a similar solvent in order to reduce the oily nature of this wood.

When the joints have been glued (photo 4) the carcase can be folded round and the ends pulled tightly together with more tape. Surplus glue should be removed with a damp cloth and the squareness tested (photo 5) before setting it

115

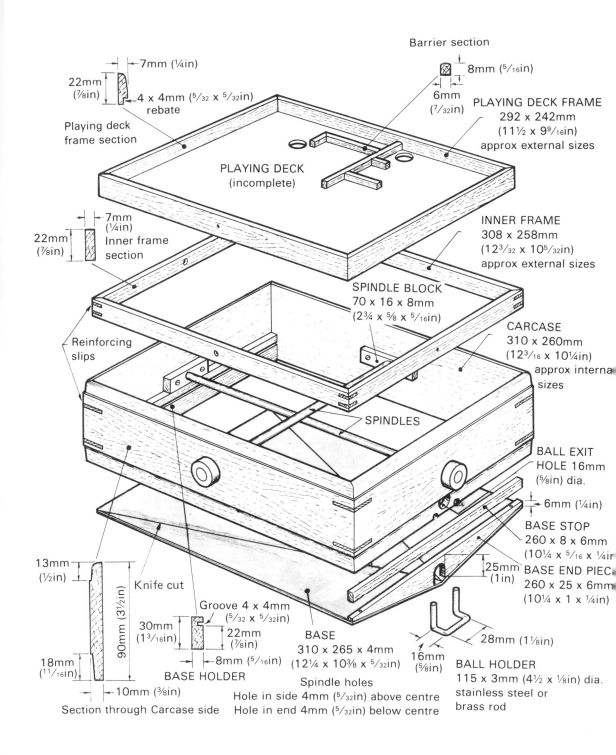

Barrier section

8mm (5/16in)

7mm (1/4in)

22mm (7/8in)

4 x 4mm (5/32 x 5/32in) rebate

Playing deck frame section

6mm (7/32in)

PLAYING DECK FRAME
292 x 242mm
(11½ x 9⁹/₁₆in)
approx external sizes

PLAYING DECK
(incomplete)

7mm (1/4in)

22mm (7/8in)

Inner frame section

INNER FRAME
308 x 258mm
(12³/₃₂ x 10⁵/₃₂in)
approx external sizes

SPINDLE BLOCK
70 x 16 x 8mm
(2¾ x 5/8 x 5/16in)

Reinforcing slips

CARCASE
310 x 260mm
(12³/₁₆ x 10¼in)
approx internal sizes

SPINDLES

BALL EXIT HOLE 16mm (5/8in) dia.

6mm (1/4in)

BASE STOP
260 x 8 x 6mm
(10¼ x 5/16 x 1/4in)

13mm (½in)

Knife cut

25mm (1in)

BASE END PIECE
260 x 25 x 6mm
(10¼ x 1 x 1/4in)

90mm (3½in)

30mm (1³/₁₆in)

Groove 4 x 4mm (5/32 x 5/32in)

22mm (7/8in)

28mm (1⅛in)

18mm (¹¹/₁₆in)

8mm (5/16in)

BASE
310 x 265 x 4mm
(12¼ x 10⅜ x 5/32in)
Spindle holes
Hole in side 4mm (5/32in) above centre
Hole in end 4mm (5/32in) below centre

16mm (5/8in)

BALL HOLDER
115 x 3mm (4½ x 1/8in) dia.
stainless steel or brass rod

BASE HOLDER

10mm (3/8in)

Section through Carcase side

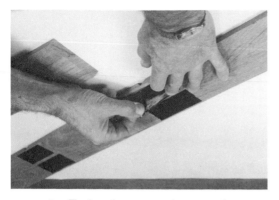

3. Taping the carcase pieces together

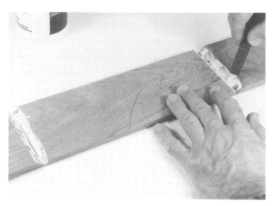

4. Gluing the mitred joints

5. Checking the squareness of the carcase

aside to dry. Any slight error of squareness can be corrected with a strip of thin wood placed diagonally between opposite corners, to provide pressure in the direction required. Mitred corners, with their relatively small area of end grain gluing, have to be stregthened if they are to survive years of constant use. Because this cannot be done internally it is necessary to glue slips of wood into slots cut across the corners. If executed with care this is not unsightly and

6. Sawing the corners to receive the reinforcing slips

can, indeed, be a decorative detail. The slots can be made with a tenon saw (photo 6), or on a circular saw with a shaped block of wood used against the carcase to tilt it at 45°. Just two circular saw cuts in each corner should give sufficient strength, but the thinner blade of the tenon saw will necessitate making three or four cuts. The depth of the cuts should be such that they almost penetrate the inner corners of the carcase. The triangular slips of wood should be a close fit in the cuts and, after gluing, they can be tapped into place (photo 7).

Inner frame

This is made in a similar way to the carcase and swivels inside it to give a gimbal action to the playing deck. The sides and ends should be cut to length on a mitre block so that they fit easily inside the carcase. The mitres can now be trimmed gradually, on a disc sander or by planing, until the frame fits inside the carcase with the necessary 1mm ($\frac{3}{64}$in bare) clearance all round. It is convenient to determine this clearance by using card or veneer packing pieces of

7. Tapping the slips into place

117

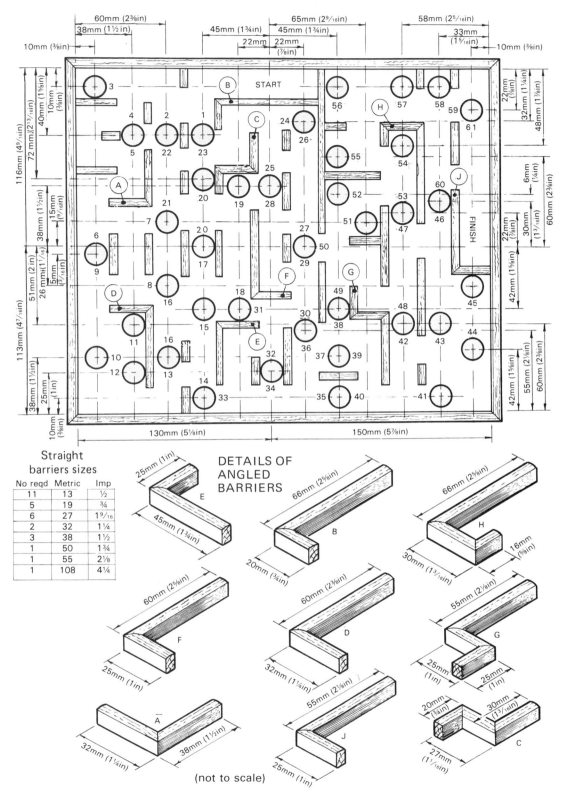

Straight barriers sizes

No reqd	Metric	Imp
11	13	½
5	19	¾
6	27	1 9/16
2	32	1¼
3	38	1½
1	50	1¾
1	55	2⅛
1	108	4¼

DETAILS OF ANGLED BARRIERS

(not to scale)

118

8. Fitting the inner frame into the carcase

10. Bevelling the inner surface of the playing deck frame

9. Rebating the playing deck frame

11. Fitting the playing deck frame

this thickness near the corners. After gluing the mitres, the frame can be replaced in the carcase and the packing pieces re-introduced to provide pressure on the joints as the glue sets (photo 8). When dry the frame should be removed with care and the rather delicate corners reinforced with slips of wood as previously described. The protruding portion of the slips in the frame and in the carcase can be sawn away with a fine-toothed backsaw, then smoothed with a block plane.

Playing deck frame

The lower inner edge of this frame is rebated to receive the playing deck, and the upper edge bevelled to complement the top edge treatment of the carcase. If the rebate is to be hand planed it is more convient to do this on a wider piece of wood (photo 9), then reduce it to the finished width later. Alternatively the rebate can be machined on with a circular saw or planer. The bevelled surface can be planed with a block plane (photo 10) to lines pencilled onto the side and edge giving its size. The corners are mitred as described for the inner frame, and to give the

same clearance (photo 11). Planing these mitred ends is not quite so straightforward because the rebated edge must not be placed against the shooting board far end stop. If it is, the end grain will be split away next to the rebate. Instead, the wood must be held against the *near* end stop and the planing done in the reverse direction. Before gluing the frame together, the upper edges should be slightly radiused to the section given with a block plane and fine abrasive paper. Because it is glued to the playing deck this frame will not require strengthening in the corners. The inside of the frame should be polished before the pre-finished playing deck is glued in place.

Carcase completion

Decorative bevelled rebates are worked onto the upper and lower edges of the carcase, to relieve the 'boxy' appearance and lighten the heavy triple thickness of the upper edges. They can be cut most easily on a circular saw with tilting blade or table, or they can be hand planed in the vice as shown (photo 12). The extent of the rebates should first be gauged onto the sides and

12. Planing the decorative rebate on the carcase

13. Drilling the ball exit hole

14. Planing the edges of the playing deck veneers

15. Spreading the glue on the playing deck

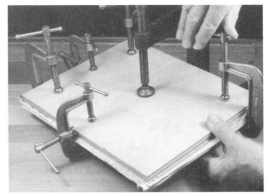

16. Cramping down the playing deck veneer

using abrasive paper wrapped over a square-edged block of wood.

The ball exit hole is bored, with a twist drill or flat bit, through the rebate at one end (photo 13). The bit should be tilted slightly to allow the hole to be bored square with the bevelled surface. Other parts which require making and fitting are the grooved base holder and its opposite end base stop, and the two hardwood blocks which receive the ends of the operating spindles. These should be screwed into place, to be accurately opposite the spindle holes drilled in the side and end of the carcase, as shown in the drawing.

Playing deck
This can be made from a piece of light coloured plywood, the type usually described as 'birch' or, to give a much improved appearance, veneered with a white coloured veneer. It is often possible to obtain sycamore veneer wide enough to cover the deck area in one piece but, if not, two pieces can be joined together edge to edge. Their edges will require planing on a

edges with a marking gauge. The bevel precludes the normal use of the rebate plane fence and it is therefore necessary to cramp a straight-edge onto the side aligned with the gauge line. It can now be planed with a normal rebate plane, or the bullnose version, as shown, working from each end to avoid splintering away the end grain of the adjacent sides. The rebates can be sanded smooth and the upper edges rounded

120

shooting board (photo 14) and during this process the leaves should be held down flat with a piece of wood with but a millimetre or two (1/16in) protruding over into the path of the plane. When an accurately fitting joint has been obtained, the edges can be pulled together and held with pieces of sellotape. The plywood for the playing deck should be prepared oversize, with the grain running *across* it, not lengthwise. Even a board of this modest size would normally be veneered on the reverse side, to stabilise it and prevent buckling and warping. However, because it is well perforated, the usual tensions are relieved and in this instance a backing veneer is not necessary.

When the glue has been spread over the ply groundwork (photo 15), and the veneer positioned over it, paper should be placed above and below the workpiece. Rectangles of thick plywood or chipboard should be G cramped into place on each side of the playing deck, to provide the necessary pressure on the veneer (photo 16). If a deep throated G cramp is not available to provide pressure near the centre of the deck, it could be gripped in a vice instead, or the veneering done in a press (see chapter 3). When dry, a cabinet scraper is the preferred tool to render the surface smooth and flat (photo 17). After sawing and planing the deck to be a good fit in its rebated frame, it can be rubbed to a fine finish with a smooth grit abrasive paper wrapped over a cork block. The hole positions can be marked onto a paper or thin card template first, then transferred onto the deck by pricking their positions through with a sharp point (photo 18).

Deck polishing
The wood finish has to be applied to the deck in two separate operations; the first to seal the surface and provide a base on which to apply the rub-down numbers, and the second to seal them permanently into place. Three wood finishes are capable of giving the required smooth surface, and the choice may depend on the availability of the materials or on the experience of the woodworker. All of them are compatible with the original rub-down numbers – Letraset – but some may react with those more recently introduced. It is prudent to test the numbers for any adverse reaction with the finish before applying either to the playing deck. An excellent finish, and one that is easy to apply, is Rustin's clear plastic coating. Two

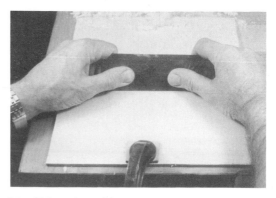

17. Using the cabinet scraper to clean up the playing deck veneer

18. Pricking through the positions of the holes in the playing deck

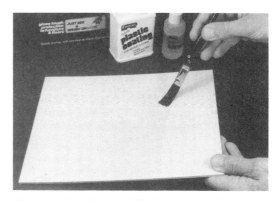

19. Applying the wood finish to the playing deck

coats should be applied (photo 19) then lightly smoothed with a very fine (400 grit) wet and dry abrasive paper, used 'wet' (photo 20). The holes can now be drilled with a flat bit (photo 21), with waste wood attached to the underside of the playing deck with double-sided tape, to avoid possible problems when the bit penetrates the lower surface. The rub-down numbers and letters can now be applied (photo 22), then two

20. Smoothing the playing deck with wet and dry abrasive paper

23. Truing the ends of the barrier pieces

21. Drilling the playing deck holes

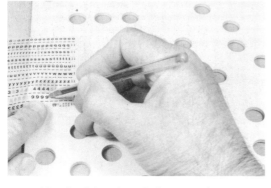

22. Applying the rub-down numbers

further coats of finish brushed on. This final coat should be lightly smoothed as before, this time on a wood block or the vulnerable edges around the holes could be abraded. Finally, it is burnished to a high gloss with the cream supplied in the polishing kit. This cream will produce a high gloss, glass-like surface which will not inhibit the smooth rolling action of the ball in any way. Similar results can be obtained, though less quickly, and with a less hardwear-

ing surface, with clear yacht varnish. The application is almost identical to that described above except that Tripoli powder is used, in place of the burnishing cream, to produce the final high gloss. The third finish is French (shellac) polish. The initial coats of this are easy to apply, being brushed on with a soft mop; after a light sanding, the rub-down numbers and letters are applied. The finishing procedures, using a rubber charged with polish, and spiriting off, are less simple and not really suitable for the inexperienced.

If preferred, the edges of the holes can be stained black with a felt tipped marker, but this should only be applied after the wood has been sealed or the colour may soak into the edges of the veneer around the hole. The polished deck can now be glued into its frame, using sellotape to pull the sides into good contact, and with the underside of the deck weighted to press it fully into the rebates.

Barriers
The upper edge of the barrier wood should be slightly radiused to the section given, using a block plane and fine abrasive paper placed on a block. The individual pieces can be sawn off slightly overlong, then pared to length with a chisel or, most conveniently, trued on a disc sander. The makeshift version of this shown (photo 23) uses an electric hand drill with abrasive paper glued to a disc of wood. The stepped wooden fence can be used to square the ends of the barriers, and also to produce the left and right hand mitres required on the angled barriers. If the square fence is marked with the lengths of the barriers, one end can be sanded until the opposite end aligns with the mark.

122

An effective method of holding the angled barriers at 90°, while the glue hardens, is to press them down onto a piece of board covered in double-sided adhesive tape (photo 24). The outer edges of the mitred corners can be held together with narrow strips of sellotape, which should be fixed in place before the glue is applied. All the straight barriers, too, can be pressed onto the 'sticky' surface, as this is a useful way to hold them as the wood finish is applied. This can be done by brushing on two or three coats of polyurethane seal or French (shellac) polish. The barriers can be levered cleanly away with a sharp knife, then glued to the deck with rapidly setting epoxy resin adhesive (photo 25). If this is done with care, and the minimum of adhesive used, it should not be necessary to clean any excess glue away afterwards.

24. Fixing the glued angled barriers to the adhesive surface

Frame pivoting
The four holes in the inner frame, to receive the pivoting screws, should be drilled to a close, but not tight, fit for the shank of the screws. These holes are countersunk on opposite sides of the frame as shown in the drawing. The playing deck frame can now be wedged inside the inner frame, with the edges of each accurately aligned as the small holes are drilled for the pivoting screws (photo 26). The same procedure should be used when drilling the holes which pivot the inner frame in the carcase.

Base
This helps to strengthen the carcase, and collects and delivers the lost ball to the replay holder. Its slightly complex form makes it difficult to shape precisely by measurement alone, and it should therefore be made a little oversize, initially, then planed to fit later. Two pencil lines are marked on the base from each corner of one end to meet in the centre of the opposite end. These lines can then be cut in deeply with a marking knife used against a straight-edge (photo 27). These cuts allow the base to be bent slightly upwards into the shallow vee shape required. This shape is maintained by gluing and G cramping it to the shaped base end piece (photo 28). Glue, well rubbed into the knife cuts, will help to strengthen the base. The base can now be reduced in size slightly until it fits into place snugly with its straightedge engaged in the retaining groove. A small screw, inserted near each corner of the opposite end, will secure the

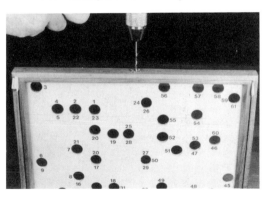

25. Gluing the barriers in position

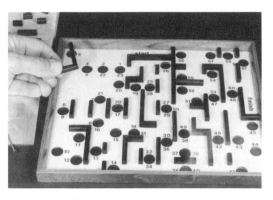

26. Drilling the pivoting screw holes

base in place against the stop.

When the ball emerges through the replay hole in the left hand end of the carcase, it is retained by a bent metal holder. This is bent to shape first, then the holes to receive it drilled to suit. The rod should be bent into a square based U-shape in a metalworker's vice, using a hammer. Vice clamps of tinplate, or other thin metal, should be used to prevent the serrated jaws of the vice from marking the rod (photo

27. Cutting along the bend lines with a marking knife

30. Bending the protruding ends to a right angle

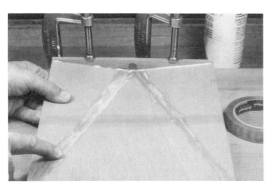

28. Gluing the base

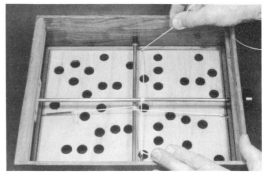

31. Tensioning and tying the operating strings

29. Bending the U-shaped ball holder

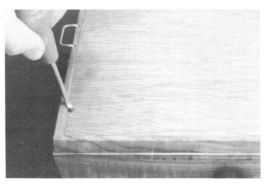

32. Fixing the base in place

29). About 16mm (⅝in) of the base of the U should now be gripped in the vice, with the two free ends projecting vertically upwards. These can now be bent to a sharp right angle as shown (photo 30). Holes to suit can now be drilled into the lower edge of the base, the correct distance apart, to suit the holder. Two holes of the same size are drilled through the rebated side to meet these holes. They accommodate the diameter of the holder rod, and allow its lower surface to be flush with the lower edge of the carcase when it is tapped in place.

Spindles and control knobs
The spindles are pieces of mild steel or brass rod with the control knobs fixed to their ends. The knobs can be purchased ready-made from hi-fi or radio component stores, or turned from suitable hardwood. Those shown were turned from discs of ebony with a recess cut in the end to receive a circle of leather used to conceal the centre hole. The centre hole, and the end of the spindle, can be threaded then secured together with epoxy resin adhesive. The spindles can be held in place with turned collars, fitted with

grub screws, or, more simply, by using several layers of adhesive tape wrapped around the spindle. A washer should be placed between each knob and the carcase, and also on the inside between the carcase and the winding of tape, or the collar, to minimise friction at these points.

Finishing

The processes not already dealt with are covered generally in chapter 4.

Assembly

Small brass screw eyes should be fixed about 10mm (³⁄₈in) off centre to the lower edge of the playing deck ends and to the sides of the inner frame. If insterted 'on' centre, the eyes may foul the spindles when the frames are in their fully tilted position in either direction. The frames can now be secured together, and to the carcase, with the pivoting screws, using washers between to maintain the correct clearance. The game can now be inverted, and each operating string attached to a small tension spring which is then anchored to a screw eye. The free end of the string should then be wrapped twice around the spindle and tensioned through the opposite eye, and tied as shown (photo 31). The base can now be screwed into place (photo 32) after testing the easy movement of the frames. Before tapping the holder in place the return action of the ball should be tested. If it 'hangs up' a small round file can be used, through the ball return hole, to smooth out any hindrances.

5 Nine Men's Morris

This ancient game, also called mill, merelles or merels, was played in Sri Lanka in 1400BC, and was popular in England in the Middle Ages when it was played on the village green. According to *Hoyles Games Modernised* (1950 edition) it could, within the last generation or so, be seen 'played by rustics in village alehouses on a chalkmarked table'!

Today, avoiding both the chalk dust and the straws in mouth, it can be played at home on an up-to-date inlaid effect board mounted on a base, with recesses for the waiting men. It is an easy, yet interesting game for two people to play; similar to Noughts and Crosses, but without its tactical limitations.

Object

In essence, the aim is to place three men in a row along any line (a mill). Taking turns, the two players place men on the board, and when there are three men in a row the player may remove (pound) one of his opponent's men, but not one in a mill, unless no other is available. Once removed from the board, the man is out of play for the rest of the game. When each player has placed all of his nine men on the board both may then move a man from its existing position to an adjoining one. A player's mill may be broken by removing a man, then re-established by replacing the man in a subsequent move. This allows him to remove an opponent's man. Play ceases when one player has been reduced to having only two men, or he is blocked from making a move by an opponent's man.

Construction

Quite straightforward, though careful cutting of the mitres on the ends of the veneer strips is essential if well aligned concentric squares are to be formed. A considerable help in making up the veneered pattern is the foolproof method described, which ensures that truly parallel veneer strips can be cut easily.

Materials

For maximum impact, the wood selected for the playing deck should contrast well with that chosen for the base. The juxtaposition of these parts, at right-angles to each other, does not accommodate any 'movement' between them and it is therefore essential that they are not only well seasoned, but have been acclimatised to the moisture content, or lack of it, of their surroundings. A realistic inlaid effect is given, at least to the layman, if the made up veneered surface matches the playing deck. In the version shown teak was used for the playing deck and for its veneered surface, glued to a plain sycamore base.

Prepared sizes

Base	$250 \times 180 \times 18$mm ($10 \times 7\frac{1}{8} \times \frac{11}{16}$in)
Playing deck	$190 \times 190 \times 10$mm ($7\frac{1}{2} \times 7\frac{1}{2} \times \frac{3}{8}$in)
Veneer	700×80mm ($28 \times 3\frac{1}{8}$in)
Veneer lines	1800×3mm ($54 \times \frac{1}{8}$in)
Marbles (18)	9 of each colour
Baize for base and to line the holes	

Method

Base

The prepared wood should be cut to length and the end grain made square and true by planing on a shooting board, or with the aid of a disc sander (see chapter 3). Its edges are slightly bevelled all round and this, too, can be done most easily and accurately on the shooting board, with a strip of wood pinned to the board to tilt it to the required angle. The end grain must be planed first (photo 1), then the sides. The upper surface can be smoothed with fine abrasive paper used on a cork block, but care should be taken not to round over any of the edges, even slightly, or this will impair its joint with the playing deck.

Playing deck

This piece of wood is veneered with wood of the same species. The lines, normally available

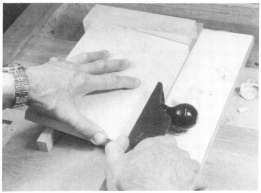

1. Bevelling the base edges on a shooting board

2. Securing the rule to the veneer with double-sided adhesive tape

in box (pale yellow) or black should be selected to contrast well with the playing deck. The wood for the playing deck should be prepared to thickness, but oversize in both length and width, and later reduced to the required size after veneering.

Veneering assembly
The strips of veneer required to make up the pattern on the playing deck have to be accurately parallel. The most reliable method to adopt in order to obtain this is to place a straightedge over the veneer and to cut along *both* edges of it. A 300mm (12in) steel rule makes an ideal straightedge, and its usual width of 25mm (1in) is ideal, although a narrower 19mm (¾in) rule could be used instead. The veneer cutting should be made with a really sharp hobby or marking knife, over a plywood or hardboard surface. Chipboard is quite unsuitable as its surface will quickly impair the cutting edge of the knife. It is helpful if the straightedge is secured to the veneer, and this can be done with a small piece of double-sided

127

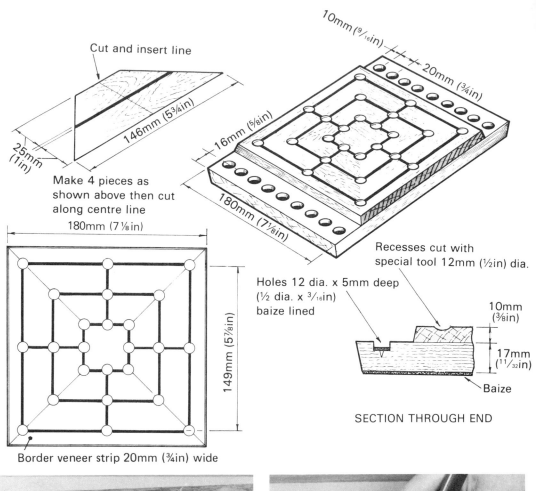

Cut and insert line

Make 4 pieces as shown above then cut along centre line

146mm (5¾in)

25mm (1in)

10mm (⁹⁄₁₆in)

20mm (¾in)

16mm (⁵⁄₈in)

180mm (7⅛in)

180mm (7⅛in)

Recesses cut with special tool 12mm (½in) dia.

Holes 12 dia. x 5mm deep (½ dia. x ³⁄₁₆in) baize lined

10mm (⅜in)

17mm (¹¹⁄₃₂in)

Baize

SECTION THROUGH END

180mm (7⅛in)

149mm (5⅞in)

Border veneer strip 20mm (¾in) wide

3. Fixing the veneer strips and lines together

4. Mitring the ends of the assembled strips

adhesive tape at each end (photo 2). Securing the straightedge in this way prevents it from moving, and makes it easier to 'change ends' when the second knife cut is made in the reverse direction. A 'line' has to be fixed between two strips of veneer, and this should be done by tensioning short pieces of sellotape into position to ensure closely abutting edges (photo

3). Brown gummed paper should now be fixed along the joint to strengthen it and to prevent glue penetrating when the veneer is glued down. The ends of the assembled strips now have to be cut to 146mm (5¾in) long with mitred ends. This can be done against a small 45° set square or a piece of thin metal cut accurately to this angle (photo 4). If several light strokes are made with the knife, the veneer should be cut through without causing it to split away at the edge. Some 'lines', particularly the boxwood variety, are quite tough and a paring action, locally, may be the most successful way of dealing with them. The mitred ends of the four pieces should now be held together to form a square, and their ends numbered to ensure identical replacement. If adjustments are necessary the mitres can be planed on a shooting board, with a firmly set block plane.

Each piece now has to be cut in half lengthwise, as accurately as possible. A sharp, fine-toothed dovetail saw can be used for this in conjunction with a mitre block, providing both sides of the veneer are reinforced with sellotape where the cut will be made. The sellotape should be peeled away on the underside when the cut has been made. Alternatively, a sharp pair of scissors could be used. Each half should now be taped back together with a short piece of line interposed between them. When the excess length of the line has been trimmed away the short piece of line can be secured to the inner edge with tape. A longer line and a strip of border veneer, both sufficiently long to enable mitres to be cut on their ends, should now be taped to the long edge. These mitres can be cut with the rule accurately aligned with the already mitred ends of the centre strips (photo 5). When assembling the four pieces, it is helpful to invert them and check their fit from the underside (photo 6). The criss-crossing tape on the under surface obscures the lines, and inaccuracies of alignment could result. The pieces should be temporarily taped together on the underside, then secured on the upper surface with brown gummed paper. When fitting the centre square of veneer it is convenient to mark its size with a sharp knife through the opening, directly onto a piece of veneer. It can then be cut with a knife against a straightedge aligned with the marks. The square should be secured in place with brown gummed paper.

Veneering

The made up sheet of veneer should be glued down to the playing deck under G cramp pressure. Two cauls – pieces of plywood, chip or blockboard – a little larger than the area to be glued are required, and also squares of paper to prevent excess glue causing a problem. The glue should be spread over the playing deck

5. Mitring the border veneer

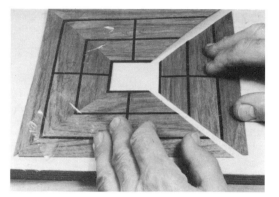

6. Checking the fit of the assembled square

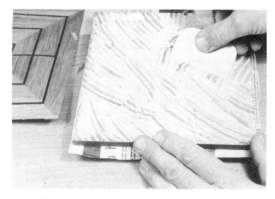

7. Spreading glue on the playing deck

(photo 7), then the veneer placed over it and taped into position. Paper should be placed over the veneer then the cauls tightened under G cramp pressure (photo 8). When dry, much of the tape on the upper surface can be removed by scrubbing with a damp cloth. The surface can now be made flat and smooth with a cabinet scraper used diagonally (photo 9), or with a medium grit abrasive paper used on a cork block. The excess size of the playing deck can

8. Gluing the veneer down under G cramp pressure

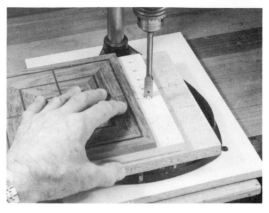

11. Drilling the marble recesses in the base, with a flat bit

9. Cleaning up the veneered surface with a cabinet scraper

12. Using a special bit to cut the marble recesses in the playing deck

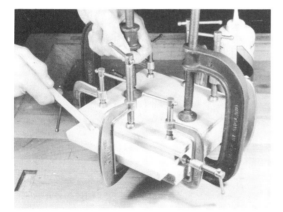

10. Gluing the playing deck to the base

now be reduced by sawing and planing until it is square and the same width as the base. The end grain edges should be bevelled on the shooting board, as for the base, then the other two edges planed.

Assembly

The playing deck should be glued to the base under G cramp pressure, using the cauls on each side as previously. The grain of the playing deck should be arranged at right-angles to that of the base, to minimise any tendency to warp. Excess glue should be removed with a sharpened stick and a damp cloth before it sets (photo 10). After sanding all surfaces smooth, a small fine piece of abrasive paper should be applied *along* the grain of the playing deck to remove scratches across the grain.

Marble recesses

The centres of the recesses in the base are marked at each end, then drilled 4mm ($\frac{5}{32}$in) deep with a 12mm ($\frac{1}{2}$in) flat bit. If possible, this should be done with a pillar drill, with the depth stop adjusted to limit the depth of each hole (photo 11). The holes in the playing deck

13.   Punching out the baize discs

can be made in the same way or, to give a better appearance, cut with a special bit to give shallow hemispherical recesses. The bit for these recesses should be made from 12mm (½in) dia. steel rod, and details of its construction are given in chapter 5 (Solitaire). Although the bit is without a point, it will indicate its centre with a small mark when rotating, if allowed to just touch the playing deck. The deck can now be moved to bring the bit to the precise position required. The depth stop can be adjusted to give even penetration of the surface with the bit or, because the bit is relatively slow in cutting, the recesses can be drilled 'by eye' to the same depth (photo 12).

Finishing
This is dealt with generally in chapter 4. Discs of baize can be fixed into the base marble holes (photo 13), and also into the playing deck holes, if these were not drilled with the special bit to give a rounded recess.

6 Noughts and Crosses

This modern version of the popular pencil and paper game is a satisfying project that is certain to revive a nostalgic interest in this competitive 'timewaster'. The apparently inlaid double cross effect is easily obtained by laminating square section blocks together with thin interleaved constrasting wood. This assembly displays the often attractive but rarely featured end grain on the playing surface. The sides of the game are framed in a contrasting wood, one edge of which is arranged to swivel to reveal storage holes for the playing marbles.

The rather 'chunky' appearance of the game is unavoidable because its size is dictated by the combined length of the column of stored marbles. Another factor is the geometry of the swivelling edge, and together these considerations determine that the sizes given are the smallest possible using the readily available 22mm (⅞in) dia. glass marbles.

Object
Each player has five marbles of one colour. The winner is the first to arrange three marbles in a line, column or diagonal. Players alternate in placing the first marble.

Construction
Difficult. The successful mitring of the corners requires that the playing area is accurately square in both planes and this is not easy to achieve. Also, to keep the overall size as compact as possible, the storage holes require quite precise drilling to give clearance to both the marble recesses and the swivelling side. Although not for the less experienced woodworker the use of power tools, particularly a disc sander, will greatly assist in the construction.

Materials
In the game shown here teak was selected for the squares, with sycamore for the 'lines' and Indian ebony for the sides. Almost any combination of timbers could be used, with contrasting ones giving the most effective appearance, but it is *essential* that they are well seasoned for this project. The swivelling edge can rotate most simply on a wood screw or, for a more satisfactory action, on a spring loaded pivot.

Prepared sizes

'Squares'	340 × 33mm sq (13½ × 1⁵⁄₁₆in sq)
'Lines'	450 × 35 × 3mm (18 × 1⅜ × ⅛in)
'Edging'	550 × 35 × 10mm (22 × 1⅜ × ⅜in)
Pivot (simple)	38mm (1½in) × 10 or 12 gauge raised head wood screw
Pivot (spring loaded)	50mm × M5 cheese-head machine screw (or similar) and nut
Spring (for above)	12–16 × 5mm (½–⅝ × ³⁄₁₆in) bore heavy gauge spring (or similar)
Marbles (10)	5 of each colour, 22mm (⅞in) dia.
Baize for base	

Method
Chequered deck
The length of prepared wood, which should be accurately square, is cut into three equal pieces. These are glued together with two thin pieces of contrasting wood in between (photo 1), checking that the surfaces of the pieces are in good alignment. If possible, the thin wood should be cut with its grain *across* its width. This will then show side grain, in place of the

1. Gluing the pieces together in the vice

2. Using large G cramps when gluing the chequered blocks together

3. Drilling the marble strorage holes

featureless end grain, on the playing surface. The sides of the blocks can now be lightly planed to just remove the protruding 'lines'. The block is now cut into three equal pieces, and two more strips of thin wood glued between them. It is convenient to do this on a flat surface to keep all the pieces in line (photo 2). Pressure can be applied with large G cramps, as shown, or by using a vice. In the latter case, use packing between the vice jaws to provide the required flat surface and to lift the workpiece up into an easily inspected position.

The top and bottom surfaces of the block must now be made flat, and with the edges square and true all round. This is most easily accomplished with a disc sander, but the surfaces can be planed; although being predominantly end-grain, this is not an easy operation. The edges will be split away if the plane is allowed to travel completely across the surface. The best procedure is to plane radially inwards all round and to lift the plane before reaching the opposite side of the workpiece. A shooting board is useful when planing the edges to ensure that they are accurately square (see chapter 3). The task of fitting the mitred edges is made much more difficult if the edges are 'out of square' in either direction.

The centres of the marble storage holes should be marked onto one edge as accurately as

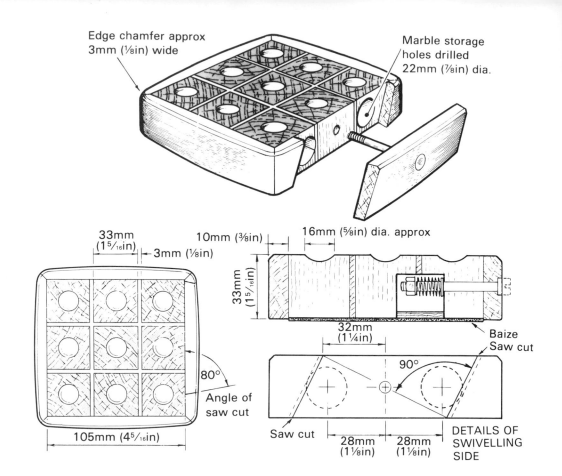

Edge chamfer approx 3mm (⅛in) wide

Marble storage holes drilled 22mm (⅞in) dia.

33mm (1⁵⁄₁₆in)

3mm (⅛in)

10mm (⅜in)

16mm (⅝in) dia. approx

33mm (1⁵⁄₁₆in)

80°

Angle of saw cut

105mm (4⁵⁄₁₆in)

32mm (1¼in)

Baize

Saw cut

90°

Saw cut

28mm (1⅛in)

28mm (1⅛in)

DETAILS OF SWIVELLING SIDE

4. Mitring the edging wood

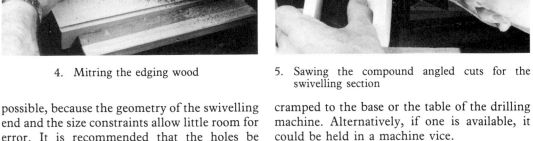

5. Sawing the compound angled cuts for the swivelling section

possible, because the geometry of the swivelling end and the size constraints allow little room for error. It is recommended that the holes be drilled with a 22mm (⅞in) dia. flat bit used in a bench drill (photo 3). The workpiece can be held firm and accurately vertical by cramping it to a square block of wood which is, itself,

cramped to the base or the table of the drilling machine. Alternatively, if one is available, it could be held in a machine vice.

Edging
Three of the edging pieces, not including the swivelling one at this stage, should have their

134

ends cut on a mitre block with a tenon saw (photo 4). To obtain perfectly fitting mitres it is usually prudent to saw them slightly long, then true them to precise length on a mitre shooting board or on a disc sander with mitre fence attachment (see chapter 3). When testing the fit of the mitres it is helpful to hold them together with sellotape. The fourth piece requires two compound angled saw cuts to be made across it before it is secured back together, as one piece, for mitring its ends. It is worthwhile nailing three pieces of wood together to make a cutting box, to ensure that identical sloping cuts are made to each end of the swivelling section (photo 5). Theoretically, at least, the sloping cut through the *thickness* of the edge assists in maintaining the contact and alignment of the cover, when closed. The sawn ends require smoothing to just remove the saw marks, and this can be done most readily on a disc sander or with a smooth cut file. If a file is used, great care must be exercised to avoid rounding the sawn edges. When the pieces are placed back together on a flat surface the joints between them should be, ideally, barely visible.

The three pieces should now be pulled into close end-to-end contact with sellotape, then fixed to a strip of wood, similar in size to the edge piece, with double-sided tape (photo 6). Held together in this way they can now be treated as a single piece of wood, as the ends are mitred and trimmed to fit around the base. When a good fit has been obtained the edging pieces should be glued except, of course, for the swivelling portion, and cramped together around the deck. Vice pressure can be used on two of the edges, and a G cramp or two used on the others (photo 7). The edging pieces, which may slide on the film of glue while being cramped, should be adjusted to overlap the underside of the playing deck to provide a recess for the baize. When removed from the cramps, the swivelling section of the edge may be fixed in place with glue which has seeped onto it from the fixed ends. This is fortuitous as it allows the outer edges to be shaped with a bandsaw or pared with a chisel, without delay. If the section is not already attached, it can be secured with a spot of glue at each end. The edges can now be smoothed, and the upper edge chamfer made, with a block plane or spokeshave. Later, after the pivot hole has been drilled, the swivelling edge can be released by a sharp tap against the bench.

6. Fixing the swivelling edge parts together onto a strip of wood

7. Gluing the edging pieces in place

Pivot

The edge can be made to swivel most easily on a wood screw, and a raised head type will give the best appearance. The hole for the shank of the screw, which should be a close fit, should be drilled through the edge and part way down into the playing deck, to ensure good alignment. If a brass screw is used, the head should be polished and lacquered to preserve its brightness. Alternatively, to provide a superior 'feel' to the turning action, and one that will not loosen with time, a spring-loaded bolt or machine screw pivot could be used. The precise diameter of the pivot is not important – within the range 4, 5 or 6mm, 2 or 4 BA, $\frac{3}{16}$ or $\frac{1}{4}$in would all be suitable – but it does require to be at least 38mm (1½in) long. A cheese-headed type is recommended. After drilling the hole for the shank, it can be *slightly* counterbored (recessed) to be a close fit for the head. The slotted outer protion of the head can now be sawn and filed away, to leave just an inlaid metal disc showing in the centre of the swivelling edge (photo 8).

A large recess, drilled with a flat or forstner

8. Showing the flush finish of the pivot bolt head

9. Tightening the knurled nut with a screwdriver

bit, is made to intercept the pivot hole to accept the washer, spring and nut. A disc of wood should be made for pressing into the recess to conceal it and to give a flat surface for the baize. Because it is not easy to engage the nut on the end of the pivot, it is helpful if some threads are drilled away on one side of the nut to help with its alignment. If some shallow slots are sawn on the edges of the nut it may be easier to tighten it with a screwdriver, or, if available, a knurled nut could be used instead (photo 9). After the game has received its final smoothing with a fine abrasive, the recessed head of the pivot can be polished with crocus paper or fine steel wool to remove scratches.

Marble recesses
These should be made with either a forstner bit or, to give a more pleasing rounded recess, with a specially made D type bit. Making a special bit, in this instance from 16mm (⅝in) dia. steel, is dealt with under 'Solitaire' in chapter 5. Using either bit, the depth of the recesses must be carefully limited or they could penetrate into the marble storage holes. For this reason, a bench or pillar drill should be used, and the depth stop or the travel of the chuck limited to give recesses just deep enough to hold the marbles securely.

Finishing
This, and securing baize to the underside, is dealt with in chapter 4.

136

7 PUZZLE SOLUTIONS

1 Black to White

To make the solution easier, the positions of the upper letter spaces are numbered 1 to 5 and the lower spaces 6 to 10. The channels which connect the two are designated LC (left channel) and RC (right channel). The listed moves specify where the letter blocks are moved *from* and where they are moved *to*. Other, and possibly quicker, solutions may be possible.

Letter	From	To	Letter	From	To	Letter	From	To	Letter	From	To
L	2	LC	K	4	RC	E	LC	7	E	4	3
B	1	2	A	3	5	E	7	8	A	RC	4
T	9	RC	L	2	4	C	2	7	L	9	RC
I	8	9	H	LC	2	H	3	2	C	8	9
H	7	8	H	2	3	H	2	LC	H	7	8
L	LC	7	I	7	2	I	4	2	I	LC	7
B	2	LC	T	8	7	T	5	3	T	2	LC
A	3	1	T	7	LC	A	RC	4	E	3	2
C	4	2	C	9	7	L	9	RC	A	4	3
T	RC	4	E	10	8	E	8	9	L	RC	4
T	4	3	K	RC	9	C	7	8	C	9	RC
I	9	4	K	9	10	H	LC	7	H	8	9
H	8	9	L	4	9	I	2	LC	I	7	8
H	9	RC	A	5	4	T	3	2	T	LC	7
L	7	9	A	4	RC	A	4	3	E	2	LC
W	6	8	H	3	5	L	RC	4	A	3	2
B	LC	7	I	2	4	E	9	RC	L	4	3
B	7	6	T	LC	2	C	8	9	C	RC	4
W	8	7	C	7	LC	H	7	8	C	4	5
W	7	LC	E	8	7	I	LC	7	L	3	4
L	9	7	L	9	8	T	2	LC	L	4	RC
H	RC	9	A	RC	9	A	3	2	A	2	4
H	9	8	I	4	RC	L	4	3	E	LC	2
I	4	9	H	5	4	E	RC	4	E	2	3
T	3	4	T	2	3	E	4	5	T	7	2
T	3	RC	C	LC	2	L	3	4	I	8	7
C	2	4	E	7	LC	L	4	RC	I	7	LC
A	1	3	L	8	7	A	2	4	H	9	7
W	LC	2	A	9	8	T	LC	2	L	RC	9
W	2	1	I	RC	9	T	2	3	L	9	8
L	7	2	H	4	RC	I	7	2	A	4	9
H	8	7	T	3	5	H	8	7	C	5	4
H	7	LC	H	RC	4	H	7	LC	C	4	RC
I	9	7	H	4	3	C	9	7	E	3	5
T	RC	9	I	9	4	L	RC	9	T	2	4
T	9	8	A	8	9	L	9	8	I	LC	2
C	4	9	A	9	RC	A	4	RC	I	2	3
K	5	4	L	7	9	E	5	4	H	7	2
						L	8	9	L	8	7
						C	7	8	A	9	8
						H	LC	7	C	RC	9
						I	2	LC			
						T	3	2			

The puzzle is completed in 160 moves.

137

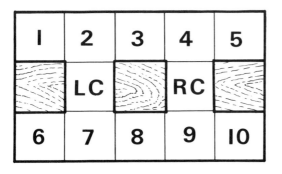

2 Board Puzzle

The solution given is for the symmetrical multi-banded pattern. The heavy lines indicate the junctions between the pieces.

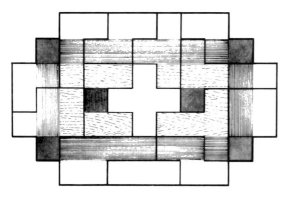

3 Boat Puzzle

The solution – as printed in 1840 – is as follows:
1. Black takes over black.
2. One of the blacks gets out, and the other returns with the boat and takes over another black.
3. Black returns with the boat and gets out.
4. White gets into the boat and takes over white.
5. One of the whites gets out; the other brings back a black.
6. Black gets out; the other black gets in and is taken over by the white.
7. Black gets out and white brings back the other black.
8. Black gets out; white gets in and is taken over by the white.
9. Both get out; black gets in and fetches over the remaining blacks one at a time.

4 Chinese Cube

Assemble the pieces together in the hand, as shown in the exploded view (drawing 1). Next,

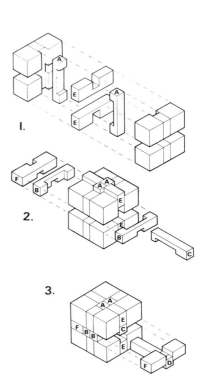

insert the two square B pieces which will help to hold the cube together. Before further pieces can be inserted, the vertical square A pieces and the rectangular E pieces must be pushed upwards as shown (drawing 2). This allows the square C piece to be inserted. Next, insert a rectangular F piece, then press the raised pieces down. This reveals a square aperture through the cube into which the square D piece can be inserted with the second rectangular F piece attached as shown (drawing 3).

5 Easy Cube

Only one solution is possible but, because the cube can be placed with any of its six sides at the bottom, it does, at first sight, give the illusion that others are possible (see first drawing on next page).

6 Five into One Square

The pieces are placed together as shown, with the hypotenuse of four large pieces and four

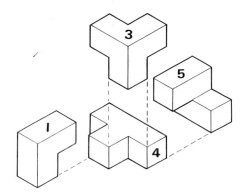

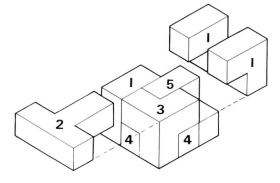

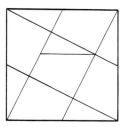

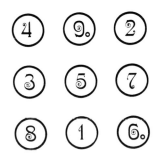

small ones making up the perimeter of the square.

7 Magic Square

The numbers are arranged as shown. It is easier to repeat the solution if it is remembered that number 5 is placed in the centre.

4	9	2
3	5	7
8	1	6

8 Puzzle Cubes

First identify the number of each cube, then its face with the line and symbol(s). Arrange these faces together in the rack with the pairs of symbols abutting as shown in the drawing.

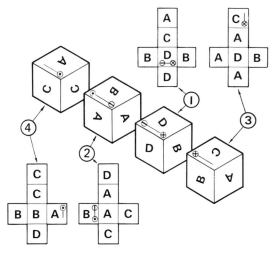

9 Number Sequence

It is not possible to give a solution to this puzzle as the starting position is not constant.

10 Six Piece Chinese Puzzle

The pieces are placed together as shown in the drawings, then piece 6 inserted to lock the pieces together.

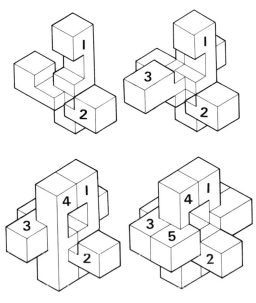

11 Steady Hand Puzzle

No solution necessary.

12 Three Piece Chinese Puzzle

The pieces are assembled as shown, then the top piece moved down until it stops. The other horizontal piece should then be pushed fully to the right, as indicated by the arrow.

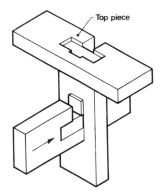

Top piece

13 Tower of Hanoi

The discs are numbered 1–7 (the smallest number 1, and the largest number 7) and the pegs A, B and C, with A the centre one and B and C at either end. Start with all the discs stacked on peg B, with the largest at the bottom.

Move	B	A	C
1		1	
2			2
3			1
4		3	
5	1		
6		2	
7		1	
8			4
9			1
10	2		
11	1		
12			3
13		1	
14			2
15			1
16		5	
17	1		
18		2	
19		1	
20	3		
21			1
22	2		
23	1		
24		4	
25		1	
26			2
27			1
28		3	
29	1		
30		2	
31		1	
32			6
33			1
34	2		
35	1		
36			3
37		1	
38			2
39			1
40	4		
41	1		
42		2	
43		1	
44	3		
45			1
46	2		
47	1		
48			5
49		1	
50			2
51			1
52		3	
53	1		
54		2	
55	1		
56			4
57			1
58	2		
59	1		
60			3
61		1	
62			2
63			1
64		7	
65	1		
66		2	
67		1	
68	3		
69			1
70	2		
71	1		
72		4	
73		1	
74			2
75			1
76		3	
77	1		
78		2	
79		1	
80	5		
81			1
82	2		
83	1		
84			3
85		1	
86			2
87			1
88	4		
89		1	
90			2
91			1
92	3		
93			1
94	2		
95	1		
96		6	
97		1	
98			2
99			1
100		3	
101	1		
102		2	
103		1	
104			4
105			1
106	2		
107	1		
108			3
109		1	
110			2
111			1
112		5	
113	1		
114		2	
115		1	
116	3		
117			1
118	2		
119	1		
120		4	
121		1	
122			2
123			1
124		3	
125	1		
126		2	
127		1	

The puzzle is completed in 127 moves.

14 Travel Solitaire

```
          1   2   3
          4   5   6
  7   8   9  10  11  12  13
 14  15  16  17  18  19  20
 21  22  23  24  25  26  27
         28  29  30
         31  32  33
```

From	Removed	To		From	Removed	To
5	10	17		21	14	7
12	11	10		10	9	8
3	6	11		7	8	9
1	2	3		30	25	18
18	11	6		28	29	30
3	6	11		33	30	25
10	11	12		31	32	33
13	12	11		18	25	30
27	20	13		33	30	25
8	9	10		16	23	28
10	11	12		25	24	23
13	12	11		28	23	16
26	19	12		17	16	15
22	15	8		4	9	16
7	8	9		15	16	17

15 Tricky Hook

As mentioned, this is a trick and not strictly a puzzle. To demonstrate the 'solution' withdraw the plunger about 30mm (1¼in) then pinch the tapered end between the forefinger and thumb. This will propel the plunger sharply back into the body of the puzzle exactly as if the hook had engaged on the elastic band. The finger and thumb can be lubricated, if necessary, by a gentle, reflective pinch of the nose!

SUPPLIERS

These suppliers in the United Kingdom will provide lists of their comprehensive range of exotic and other hardwoods and veneers. Please enclose a stamped addressed envelope with enquiries.

Hardwoods
North Heigham Sawmills
Paddock Street
Norwich NR2 4TW
Tel: 0603-22978

Veneers
Art Veneer Co Ltd
Industrial Estate
Mildenhall
Suffolk IP28 7AY
Tel: 0638-712550

ACKNOWLEDGEMENTS

I should like to record my grateful thanks to the many people who have helped in the preparation of this book. In particular to my wife and amanuensis, Mary, and to Audrey Dopson for her prompt and faultless typing of the manuscript. Also Philip Cleverley, who prepared the drawings, Ray Dopson, Arthur Fletcher, Marilyn Page, Julia Higby and Rebecca Quew. To my children, Jane and Peter, who helped in various ways, and to Anthony, aged eight, who solved two puzzles which defeated me!

I am also indebted to Harry Wicks, workshop editor of *Popular Mechanics*, for allowing me to include work of mine, on puzzles, which was first published in that magazine; and to Brio-Scanditoy for supplying details of their unique 'Labyrintspel' game and for giving permission for its inclusion.

Finally, but certainly not least, to Sue Viccars of David & Charles for her efficient and friendly help in the production of this book.

Technical Note

All the black and white photographs, except those in chapter 3, were taken on *Ilford* FP4 film and printed on *Ilfospeed*.